Teacher Agency
and
Curriculum Making
in
Classrooms

D1570755

TEACHER AGENCY
AND
CURRICULUM MAKING
IN
CLASSROOMS

Cynthia L. Paris

Teachers College, Columbia University
New York and London

Published by Teachers College Press, 1234 Amsterdam Avenue,
New York, New York

Copyright © 1993 by Teachers College, Columbia University

Library of Congress Cataloging-in-Publication Data

Paris, Cynthia L.
    Teacher agency and curriculum making in classrooms / Cynthia L.
Paris.
        p.   cm.
    Includes bibliographical references and index.
    ISBN 0-8077-3225-7
    1. Teacher participation in curriculum planning—United States.
    2. Education, Elementary—United States—Curricula—Case studies.
    I. Title.
    LB2806.15.P37   1993   92-34554
    372. 19—dc20

ISBN 0-8077-3225-7

Printed on acid-free paper
Manufactured in the United States of America
99 98 97 96 95 94 93   7 6 5 4 3 2 1

Contents

INTRODUCTION

In the past decade, educators, legislators, and child and family advocates have called for greater participation of teachers in curriculum matters. They hold that teachers' active engagement with curriculum will professionalize teaching (Holmes Group, 1986; Shanker, 1986; Sizer, 1984), ensure higher quality education for all children (Bastian, Fruchter, Gittel, Greer, & Haskins, 1986; National Coalition of Advocates for Students, 1985), and improve the productivity of schools and the nation (National Governors Association, 1986; Carnegie Forum on Education and the Economy, 1986). Together, they assert that educational reform requires participation of teachers who are both capable and empowered as active agents in curriculum work. The gap between teachers' current relationships to curriculum and the active relationships described by reformers, however, is wide.

Teachers' engagement with curriculum is typically limited to implementing a curriculum that was created or selected for them by others. Mathematics teaching is a case in point. As described by Romberg (1988), it is preponderantly a textbook-driven process in which teachers do not vary the content, method, or sequence of the curriculum dictated by a required text. Gitlin (1983) and Apple (1986) describe teachers' similarly limited engagement with curriculum when schools employ prescriptive and labor-intensive mastery learning and individualized learning programs. It may be unrealistic to assume, therefore, that the majority of teachers currently in the schools—who were trained to teach prescriptive teacher-proof, textbook-based curricula and were usually rewarded for accepting and implementing the curricula of others—will be prepared or willing to take on more empowered roles in relation to curriculum. It may be equally unrealistic to assume that new teachers, many of whom have been systematically trained in teacher education programs for "deskilled" positions requiring merely implementation of curriculum (Ginsburg, 1988; Huling-Austin, 1990), will be prepared or willing to take active and effective roles in curriculum work.

There are, however, teachers who have actively engaged in the creation and critique of curriculum in their own classrooms. Long before reformers' calls for teacher participation in curriculum making and the radical reform of schools, teachers responded to curricula they deemed inadequate or inappropriate for their students by embellishing it, reorganizing it, or rejecting it

1

entirely and holding fast to curricula that they had tested and refined over years. Similarly, teachers have long created curricula outside the sanctioned content in order to respond to the needs and interests of their students. When their work was noticed, it was the bane of curriculum writers and administrators who sought standardization and faithful implementation of prescribed curricula. More often, however, their work went unrecognized, either through administrative oversight or through the teachers' own efforts to cover their activities. Ironically, it is among teachers characterized as "renegades" or "conservative obstructors" of curriculum change that we find models of active engagement with curriculum. Their work holds answers to questions about teachers' ability to create and critique curriculum, and how and under what conditions they do so. It is the work of such teachers that is the focus of this book.

The chapters that follow are based on a close examination of the work of four public elementary school teachers who, as participants in a university-based study of microcomputers and children's writing development, created their own word-processing curricula and adapted their existing curricula to accommodate and take advantage of word processing. What appeared to be a rather modest instance of teacher agency in an admittedly peripheral curriculum area proved to be a window onto the teachers' active intellectual engagement with curriculum—whether created by themselves or created and mandated by others. In addition to providing evidence that teachers are indeed capable of effective and professionally responsible curriculum making, this study identifies multiple and often conflicting contexts in which the teachers conducted their work, traces the processes of their curriculum work over two years, and reinterprets some much-maligned behaviors attributed to teachers in the face of curriculum change, such as questioning, cooptation, and conservatism.

The assumptions that guided the design of the study serve as a useful frame for organizing the book as well. (See the Appendix for a detailed description of the research methodology.) First, the research design and reporting assume the situated nature of experience and understanding. Part I locates teacher agency in historical and contemporary realities. Its introductory section traces the shift in teachers' roles, from active engagement with curriculum early in this century to teachers' disempowered, deskilled relationships to curriculum in the second half of the century, and outlines the organizational obstacles that have built up around the teachers' curriculum work. In Chapter 1, contemporary conceptions of teachers' relationships to curriculum are examined in light of current reform efforts, and the term *agency* is defined.

Chapter 2, which introduces the reader to the four public elementary school teachers whose experiences and perceptions follow, is grounded in the assumption that each participant "sees" events differently and assigns different meanings to what is seen. Although the personal, subjective perceptions of one participant's curriculum work may or may not match another's equally subjective view of that work, it is each teacher's internal reality that informs his or her work (Erickson, 1986). Understanding the teachers' work as active agents in curriculum matters thus requires that the meanings the teachers ascribe to events, procedures, policies, and procedures be given precedence in any analysis; throughout the book, therefore, contexts are described from the teachers' perspectives wherever possible. Curriculum processes are given meaning through the teachers' experiences, histories, goals, and values.

This study also assumes that teachers' curriculum work is a highly contextualized enterprise and, therefore, locates teacher agency in curriculum matters in its complex and often conflicting contexts. Grundy (1987) and Connelly and Clandinin (1988) argue that curriculum work, like all activity, is grounded in history, and that the ability to understand that work is dependent upon an understanding of its history. Further, Grundy (1987) and Apple (1979) argue that curriculum must be understood as an expression of ideology. To that end, Part II examines the multiple, interacting, and embedded contexts surrounding the teachers' curriculum work and traces these contexts back in time and down into underlying ideologies. The introductory section grounds the chapters that follow in prior studies of the interaction of context and practice in schools and argues for a relationship between context and practice that is neither linear nor unidirectional but, instead, is interdependent and compounding over time. In Chapter 3, the policies, practices, and dominant ideologies of the school district, school building, and the research project are documented in the past and the present. Chapter 4 examines the teachers' personal ideological contexts, particularly their assumptions about the nature of curriculum, the nature and genesis of curriculum knowledge, and the nature of curriculum change. Points at which the teachers' ideologies were in conflict with or were consonant with the policies, practices, and ideologies of those in surrounding contexts are examined in Chapter 5.

Finally, it is assumed that curriculum change is neither an event nor a unitary, generalizable process but rather a confluence of many ongoing processes. Part III documents the multiple and evolving processes that characterized the teachers' curriculum work. The introduction establishes the inadequacy of existing models of curriculum making and implementation for describing and explaining the teachers' curriculum work. The remainder of the section constructs an alternative frame for understanding the teachers' active engagement in curriculum work. Grounded in the teachers' experiences and consistent with their assumptions about curriculum knowledge, curriculum, and teachers' roles, this perspective reflects the meanings the teachers ascribed to the processes of curriculum making and curriculum change.

Chapter 6 locates the foundations of the teachers' curriculum work in the teachers' past experiences with curriculum change and in their ongoing curriculum practices. Descriptions of the teachers' initial work with word processing, which could be interpreted as expressions of conservatism or resistance, are interpreted through the lenses of the teachers' assumptions and experiences. Chapter 7 details the teachers' engagement in the often contemporaneous processes of questioning, observing, and altering their emerging curricula and their recursive and episodic progress through these processes. The Conclusion refines and expands the definition of agency and considers implications for those who would support teachers' empowerment as active agents in curriculum matters.

This book provides a picture of teacher agency as it currently exists in four elementary classrooms. It identifies conditions that have permitted and, in some cases, encouraged agency, as well as those conditions that have impeded or limited its growth. The profound influence of the historical and ideologicial contexts surrounding the teachers' work in this setting and the meanings each teacher brought to and made of their work in this setting, however, make generalization to other teachers and other schools inappropriate. This work provides, instead, a frame for seeing and understanding agency as it already exists in classrooms today and for supporting teachers' growth toward agency as it could be in schools tomorrow.

Part I
AGENCY

Teacher agency in curriculum making is not new. Long before the commission reports of the 1980s called for teacher empowerment and professionalization in matters of curriculum and policy, teachers engaged as active agents in the creation and critique of curriculum in school districts, in schools, and in their own classrooms. Early in this century, teachers in Dewey's Laboratory School met weekly to build and assess a curriculum organized around the principles set forth by Dewey (Mayhew & Edwards, 1936). Teachers in McDonald County, Missouri, created project curricula that were "continuously made on the spot by the joint action of pupils and teacher" (Kilpatrick, 1923, p. xx). In Winnetka, Illinois, teachers set school district curriculum goals and generated curricula to meet those goals through "rigorous analysis of their objectives and experiences" (Washburne & Marland, 1963, p. 20) and research in their own classrooms. Denver teachers, in collaboration with curriculum experts, determined curriculum content and organization through the study of research and their own experimentation (Newlon & Threlkeld, 1926) and brought national attention to the active participation of teachers in curriculum work (Kliebard, 1987).

Since that time, however, a confluence of events and changing ideologies has challenged the conception of teachers as participants in the creation and critique of curriculum and has had a lasting influence on thinking about the nature and genesis of curriculum knowledge. The increasing proportion of women in the teaching force (Apple, 1986), the drive for social efficiency and the simultaneous rise of scientific curriculum making, as well as the challenges to belief in the centrality of the child in curriculum making (Kliebard, 1987) altered teachers' relationship to curriculum in fundamental ways.

Between 1900 and 1930, women accounted for increasingly greater proportions of the teaching force; their numbers rose from about 60% in 1900 to nearly 90% in 1930 (Apple, 1986). With expanding work opportunities for young men and growing numbers of students enrolled in the schools, more and more young middle-class women chose, and were encouraged, to teach during this period. Judd (1926) argued that "un-trained and inexperienced girls of the type which one usually finds in charge of elementary classrooms" (p. 126) were not to be entrusted with the task of curriculum making. Accompanying the increasing feminization of the teaching force, then, was the transformation of teachers' curriculum work into a highly rationalized and controlled enterprise in which the content and method of teaching were prescribed by others (Apple, 1983, 1986).

Charges of inefficiencies in the schools (Kliebard, 1987) also contrib-uted to the rationalization and control of curriculum. Swelling ranks of social efficiency advocates argued that each child should be educated according to his or her abilities and predicted role in life, thus eliminating the wasted time and effort involved in presenting curriculum that might be too difficult for many children or might never be used. Simultaneously, the new science of mental measurement promised to determine students' abilities, and scientific management procedures for analyzing adult tasks permitted the identification of discrete and sequential behaviors to be taught. Franklin Bobbitt's "scientific technique" for curriculum making yielded "numerous, definite, and particularized" objectives that determined the curriculum or "series of experiences which children and youth must have by way of attaining those objectives" (quoted in Kliebard, 1987, p. 116). During this period someone other than the classroom teacher determined not only what was to be taught, and when and how it was to be taught, but also to whom it was to be taught.

Further blows to teachers' active relationship to curriculum came in the form of the growing belief that society's requirements, rather than the interests and needs of the individual child, should guide curriculum making. Curriculum built on knowledge of the individual child's needs and strengths was clearly in the purview of the teacher. However, curriculum that addressed society's needs, inferred from scientific analysis of adult life and tasks, was in the domain of experts working outside the classroom. The Committee on Curriculum-Making, chaired by Harold Rugg, declared that "the classroom teacher does not have at his [sic] disposal the data which are necessary" (Committee on Curriculum-Making, 1926, p. 26) nor "the time nor the training to make a scientific analysis and interpretation" (p. 27) of such data. Rugg argued further that curriculum specialists were required to "aid the teacher by cooperating with her in the planning, at least in outline, of the proposed activities and expected outcomes for the work of the school" (Rugg, 1926, p. 158).

The statement of the Committee on Curriculum-Making reflected the tension created by the converging influences on teachers' relationship to curriculum. On the one hand, the authors argued that "because of partially equipped teachers and of heavy teaching programs, large classes and inadequate research facilities, it will be necessary to utilize persons specially trained and experienced in the study of society and of childhood to organize suggestive activities, readings and exercises" (p. 20). The document's authors conceded, however, that "no formulated scheme . . . made out in advance, and handed out complete by the curriculum-maker, can, of itself be sufficient" without being supplemented with "daily life-situations and interests" determined by the learner and the teacher (p. 20). Although the committee reserved some curriculum work for the teacher, it was what Freedman (1988) has identified as gendered work, which assigns the cognitive portions or the "head" of curriculum work to the curriculum expert, who is most often male, and the affective portions or the "heart" of such work to the teacher, who is most often female.

Shifting from his previous position, Bobbitt cautioned that the scientization of education threatened the confidence of teachers in curriculum matters. Foreseeing the effects of what scholars later would identify as the "deskilling" of teaching (Apple, 1982), he argued that "there should be no mystification of the profession by specialists in scientific technique" (Bobbitt, 1926, p. 50). He argued further that "every competent teacher can have a full command over the fundamental educational science and that he [sic] must have it in order that he be competent" (p. 50). However, in the decades that followed, Bobbitt's cautions remained largely unheeded. By midcentury, curriculum had come to refer to a stable and reified product separate from and requisite to teachers' work—as opposed to an evolving process negotiated between teacher and child. The relationship of teachers to curriculum was reduced to the receiving and implementing of curricula by teachers without their having engaged intellectually in their creation or critique.

From his vantage point in the 1970s, Charles Silberman (1970) looked back on the 1950s and 1960s and characterized those decades as a time of backlash curriculum reform against the "intellectual flabbiness" (p. 170) of the curriculum of the previous decades. Curriculum scholars joined content scholars to create curricula that would allow "scholars to speak directly to the child" (p. 181). The curriculum reformers of the 1950s and 1960s, Silberman explained,

> not content with ignoring the classroom teacher . . . in effect tried to bypass the teacher altogether. Their goal, sometimes stated, sometimes implicit, was to construct "teacher-proof" curricula that would "work" whether teachers liked the materials or not or taught them well or badly. . . . They viewed teachers, if they thought of them at all, as technicians. (p. 181)

Mastery learning packages such as DISTAR, which provide teachers with scripted lessons to read to children (complete with cues to pause and smile), and computer software packages, which claim to provide instruction far superior to that provided by teachers, are among the more recent curriculum developments cited by Smith (1986) as efforts to distance the teacher still further from curriculum work.

In addition to the trend toward controlling and minimizing teachers' curriculum work through rationalized curriculum materials, state, federal, and judicial control over education tightened from the mid-1960s through the mid-1970s (Wise, 1979). Minimum competency testing, equal opportunity legislation, state-level educational standards, and accountability laws were among the myriad legislative and judicial means used during the decade to control what and how children learn and teachers teach. Curriculum at state and school-district levels was hyperrationalized or standardized in an effort to demonstrate compliance with judicial and legislative requirements for equity, efficiency, and effectiveness, thus further minimizing teachers' engagement in curriculum making and critique in their own classrooms and in schools.

It was in this historical and ideological climate that the national commissions and political action groups of the 1980s called for the participation of teachers as active agents in curriculum matters. And it was in this setting that the teachers in this study conducted their curriculum work.

1 Teacher Agency and Curriculum

The first wave of response to calls for reform did little to increase teachers' authority in curriculum matters (Apple & Jungck, 1990; Carnegie Forum, 1986; Futrell, 1986). In contradiction to the stated goal of professionalizing teaching, state initiatives subsequent to the publication of the reform reports further restricted teachers' discretion in curriculum matters. In the year following the publication of *A Nation at Risk* (National Commission on Excellence in Education, 1983), for example, 22 states mandated curriculum changes that dictated to teachers *what* topics would be taught and, in some cases, *when* topics would be taught as well (National Coalition of Advocates for Students [NCAS], 1985). Wise (1988) documented the efforts of states to increase their control over education at the local level by legislating "outcomes through standardized test, content through curriculum alignment, and teaching methods through teacher evaluation criteria" (p. 330). He renewed his earlier call for the exercise of professional discretion at the local level and argued that "the appropriateness of instruction . . . must be determined in context . . . [and] cannot be prescribed in advance of the interaction between [teacher and child]" (p. 332).

TEACHERS AND CURRICULUM DECISION MAKING

The second wave of reform has been marked by what McDonald (1988) identified as "the emergence of the teacher's voice." Whereas in the first wave of reform teachers were portrayed as "dumb instruments of school policy" (p. 471), in the second wave teachers have come to be characterized as the "chief agents of reform" (p. 471). Much attention has been directed toward restructuring schools in ways designed to increase teachers' participation in decision making. But from the perspectives of individual classroom teachers, thus far school restructuring efforts have not significantly altered either their relationships to curriculum or their roles in curriculum change. The prevailing interpretations of the terms *participation* and *curriculum decision making* bear closer examination.

9

Participation

To date, teacher participation in curriculum matters has most often been indirect, restricted to representation on committees charged with the selection or creation of curriculum. Curriculum committees at the level of the school district or the individual school, comprised of administrators and teachers who have volunteered or been appointed to represent their colleagues, thus adopt, create, or revise curricula for a school or school district. Viewing curriculum work from the macro perspectives of state school boards, school districts, or individual schools, teachers have indeed been included in "significant decisions in pedagogy" as recommended by the Holmes Group and others. However, from the perspective of the classroom teacher, teacher representation on curriculum committees does not necessarily professionalize or alter individual teachers' relationships to curriculum. The individual classroom teacher who did not serve on the committee, or the committee representative who held a minority opinion, is still expected to implement curricula created or selected by someone other than herself. She has been neither empowered nor professionalized.

Curriculum making by consensus only mimics empowerment and, in fact, may disguise the lack of power that individual teachers—even those serving on the committees—actually have in curriculum matters. Grundy (1987) warns that even "consensus arrived at through open debate and deliberation . . . can be used as a form of manipulation" when "powerful interests are participating in the meaning-making and agreement process" (p. 17). When these conditions exist, and they very well may exist whenever administrators are chairs or members of curriculum committees, there is a very real possibility that "participants deceiv[e] themselves about the real meaning of the situation" (p. 17) and are thereby subjugated rather than professionalized. Mock participation and false consensus mean that "empowered" teachers again face the day-to-day reality of implementing curriculum created or selected by others, and also struggle with their discontent with curriculum that they themselves have "participated" in fashioning. Whether teachers assert their seemingly illogical and hardly persuasive discontent (after all, "they" were the ones who chose or created the curriculum) or never express it because they have been convinced of their own complicity, the relationships of classroom teachers to curriculum have not changed. In spite of being invited to participate in curriculum processes, teachers remain receivers and implementors of curriculum created or selected by others rather than active agents in the creation and critique of curriculum.

Decision Making

Just as teacher participation in curriculum work has often been limited to participation by representation, so has curriculum decision making too often been limited to the selection of published curricula. Typically, a curriculum committee is convened and charged with the task of evaluating published curricula and selecting the one that most closely matches the goals of the school or school district. Even those committees given charges broad enough to permit the creation of curriculum are often bound by the expectation that what they produce will resemble most published curricula in form and generalizability. Local expectations and time limitations often preclude deliberation on the ends to which curriculum and teaching are directed and by-pass discussion of what knowledge is of most worth. These fundamental curriculum decisions are implicit in the goals of the school or district and in the published curricula that curriculum committees are to select or emulate; as a result, they are not open to challenge or revision.

Applying the label "curriculum decision making" to the process of selecting from among published curricula, or even to the creation of a local packaged curriculum, not only limits the nature and extent of teachers' real involvement in curriculum matters, it also sanctions this work as the product of professionalized and empowered teachers. Furthermore, it privileges curriculum decisions made outside the classroom while failing to acknowledge, and thereby devaluing, the myriad curriculum choices and critiques in which teachers engage in their day-to-day work in classrooms.

When participation in curriculum matters is interpreted to mean representation on curriculum committees that determine the general curriculum required of all teachers, and decision making is equated with selection from among published curricula, teachers' existing relationships to curriculum are reproduced rather than altered. Granting prerogative to a few individuals to make curriculum decisions for their colleagues does not alter the individual classroom teacher's relationship to the curriculum in any significant way. Furthermore, it replicates the conditions that produced the curriculum that was to be improved and preserves, unchallenged, the assumptions about curriculum and teachers on which existing curriculum practices are based.

ASSUMPTIONS ABOUT CURRICULUM AND TEACHERS

To avoid replicating past curriculum practices and reproducing the disempowered relationship of teachers to curriculum, it is necessary to examine some of the assumptions that underlie and limit thinking about teachers, curriculum, and reform. The first is the unquestioned belief that curriculum knowledge—knowledge of what to teach and how to teach it—is scientific knowledge, discovered by curriculum experts using methods and prior knowledge that are inaccessible to the typical classroom teacher. Both curriculum and the curriculum knowledge on which it is based are assumed to be created outside of, and antecedent to, implementation in an individual teacher's classroom. When curriculum making is conceived of as separate from and requisite to curriculum implementation, then the classroom teacher, the implementor, is effectively defined out of the curriculum-making process.

Teachers, Sullivan (1975) asserted, have had little experience in curriculum making and are consequently unprepared to participate in the creation and evaluation of curriculum. Similarly, Walker (1978) argued that it was unrealistic to assume that teachers could take the role of curriculum developer. More recently Rosow and Zager (1989), addressing school administrators, argued that it is fallacious to assume that teachers "should be involved in decision-making about their work because they are 'the experts' with respect to their jobs" (p. 16). They asserted that teachers, like all workers, "are far from knowing all the facts about their problems or all the possible solutions from which they can choose" (p. 67). While the authors conceded that "even today's teachers are capable of contributing much more than they are now permitted to do" (p. 20), they cautioned that "when teachers are offered the opportunity to recommend or carry out decisions regarding . . . curriculum, textbooks, [and] new forms of instruction" (p. 67) they will require careful guidance and supervision in even these most limited forms of curriculum work. They argued further that "although teachers would rather make their own mistakes and receive advice of their own choosing" (p. 67), the guidance and supervision of more knowledgeable experts should be provided. This advice and these paternalistic cautions reveal many assumptions about the knowledge and skills that teachers are thought to lack. Evidence of teachers' existing curriculum knowledge and expertise is not sought; it is simply assumed not to exist.

Proceeding on the assumption that teachers lack both the knowledge and the ability to acquire the knowledge necessary to make curriculum decisions, Walker, Sullivan, and others advocate practices that replicate the existing hierarchical relationships that place the predominantly female teaching force under the control of the more knowledgeable administrative force, which is predominantly male. In a critical review of the history of teacher education, Ginsburg (1988) notes that it is the assumed inferiority of the predominantly female teaching force that must be implicated in the reproduction of hierarchical relations based on gender. As long as teachers are assumed to be incapable of generating and critiquing curriculum knowledge, efforts to empower and professionalize teachers by inviting their "participation in curriculum decision making" will merely reproduce their existing relationships to curriculum as its receivers and implementors.

Assumptions about curriculum and teachers that limit curriculum reform are to be found in the language of those who advocate greater teacher participation as well as those who caution of its dangers. Maeroff (1988), writing in support of the empowerment of teachers, advocates the safeguard of "consultation with authorities" such as "college professors and other subject experts" if the "risk" of giving teachers "more control over curriculum development" (p. 55) is taken. He expresses doubt that teachers, thrust into positions that require curriculum decision making, "can really plan a proper curriculum" (p. 55). Maeroff argues convincingly that teachers need to be knowledgeable as well as empowered. He then describes a model program that he claims empowered teachers through its "delivery system" of curriculum knowledge. A cadre of teachers, taught by university experts, were returned to their school districts to become "presenters" of knowledge to their colleagues. In this model, teachers were cast in the roles of transmitters and receivers, rather than initiators, of curriculum work. Although I concede his point that knowledge is empowering, I challenge Maeroff's conception that curriculum knowledge can originate only from curriculum experts and also his assumption that even when teachers are merely conduits for that knowledge, they are empowered by it. Like participation by representation on curriculum selection committees, this practice assumes that curriculum knowledge is generated outside teachers' classrooms by experts, necessitating its "delivery" to teachers. Furthermore, Maeroff's model assumes a hierarchical power relationship built on curriculum experts' having and giving privileged curriculum knowledge to teachers, and it maintains teachers in the disempowered positions of receivers or deliverers of curriculum knowledge rather than its creators or critics.

The limitations of unquestioned assumptions about curriculum and teachers can also be found in the Holmes Group's (1986) proposal. In their outline of differentiated teaching roles they propose that Career Professionals, who would represent the top fifth of the teaching population, may choose, among their other responsibilities, to specialize in curriculum development. Later in the document this specialization is referred to as "curriculum improvement" (p. 40), leaving it unclear as to whether it would be within the purview of Career Professionals to create curriculum or if they would merely enhance what already exists. Because the roles described for the rest of the teaching force do not include curriculum making—Professional Teachers might engage in curriculum evaluation, but a Novice's only involvement in curriculum work would be in implementing a curriculum under the watchful eye of a Career Professional (pp. 38–39)—it might be assumed that the curriculum created or improved by the top one-fifth of the teaching force would be delivered to, and received and implemented by, the remaining teachers. This criticism is not to be taken as a denial that some teachers, by virtue of experience, education, or native talents, surpass others in the quality of their curriculum work. It is, however, meant to question the assumption that the only valid curriculum knowledge is that created by an elite group of Career

Professionals and experts in the curriculum field and that teachers cannot and do not routinely engage in curriculum work.

Failure to examine assumptions about curriculum and teachers not only limits the ways in which teachers' engagement in curriculum work might be conceived, but also limits efforts to assess the curriculum knowledge and experience teachers may actually possess. The Carnegie Foundation's 1988 survey of teacher involvement in decision making provides one example of this. The nationwide survey of over 20,000 teachers, representing all 50 states, revealed what were deemed to be discouraging levels of teacher involvement in educational decision making. The highest levels of involvement were found in "shaping the curriculum" at the school level (63% nationally, ranging from 40% in Louisiana to 85% in Vermont) and "choosing textbooks and instructional materials" at the school level (79% nationally, ranging from 61% in Maryland to 93% in Vermont). However, the use of these terms here—*involvement, shaping,* and *choosing*—is problematic. By failing to distinguish between curriculum decisions made by a member of a curriculum committee for the entire faculty and curriculum decisions made by an individual teacher for her own students, it is not clear whether choosing curriculum materials was assumed by either the survey designers or the teachers responding to be an organizational or individual task. Furthermore, the terms *involvement* and *shaping* do not distinguish between evaluating existing curricula, adopting a prepared curriculum, adapting or revising curricula, creating curricula, and evaluating or setting curriculum goals, nor do they distinguish between participation as an occasional event or an ongoing process. Not only does the failure to examine the assumptions underlying the questions limit the usefulness of the Carnegie Foundation survey as a measure of teachers' relationship to curriculum in the first wave of reform, it also indicates a troubling assumption of agreement on the meanings of these terms by a major advocate of reform.

Relying on unexamined assumptions about the nature of curriculum and teachers' relationships to it—particularly those accumulated in an era of rationalization of teaching and deskilling of teachers (Apple, 1983; Apple & Teitelbaum, 1986)—limits our vision of what may be possible and, in fact, what already may be. Furthermore, existing language and conceptions of curriculum and teachers' relationship to curriculum do not adequately describe or lead to an understanding of teacher agency in curriculum matters nor do they adequately inform those who would support the curriculum work of teachers. We need to "see" past the prevailing assumptions of the rationality of curriculum and the inferiority of teachers' curriculum knowledge in order to explore the possibilities of professionalization and empowerment of teachers.

AGENCY: ALTERNATE CONCEPTIONS
OF TEACHERS AND CURRICULUM

Alternative conceptions of curriculum, and of teachers' roles in relation to curriculum, are to be found in a small but growing collection of writings by and about teachers engaged in the research, design, and critique of curriculum in their own classrooms. Their work, and the assumptions that underlie it, challenge rather than reproduce teachers' existing relationships to curriculum. Such work offers an enlarged vision of curriculum and of teachers' knowledge and capabilities.

Representative of this body of work is that of Elbaz (1983) and Yonemura, Colletti, and Collins (1986), who document the practical knowledge, values, and beliefs of individual teachers engaged in creating, critiquing, and adapting curriculum. Similarly, Lightfoot's (1983) portraits of teachers in "good high schools" reveal the teachers to be students of curriculum, bringing considerable intellect and skill to curriculum problem solving. Teachers' accounts of their own curriculum deliberations and actions are particularly powerful. For example, Goswami and Stillman (1987) edited a collection of essays that contains work by teachers researching their own curriculum and teaching. Cochran-Smith and Lytle's collection (1993) includes teachers' descriptions of constructing and reconstructing their curricula based on their work in communities of teacher researchers. Newman's (1990) wide-ranging and moving collection of 20 teachers' essays represents the "voices of colleagues engaged in mutual struggle" (p. xv) to create and examine curricula in light of their commitment to educational excellence.

This body of work illustrates a relationship between the individual teacher, the curriculum, and curriculum knowledge that challenges dominant conceptions. In these cases, teachers created curriculum knowledge and curriculum materials through individual and collaborative research and deliberation. They did not merely receive and implement curriculum created by others, but instead made reasoned, self-conscious curriculum decisions in response to their evaluation of the needs and interests of their students and a shared commitment to educational excellence. In all cases the teachers were instrumental in curriculum work, rather than instruments in the work of others. And in all cases their work resulted in successful and effective curriculum reform, thereby challenging the assumption that teachers lack the requisite knowledge and skill to do curriculum work.

This work challenges narrow conceptions of curriculum as a rationalized product created outside of classrooms by experts and delivered to teachers for implementation. The assumption that a curriculum is a mutual and evolving creation of teacher and learners in a specific context, and that teachers are central participants in its creation and critique, invites consideration of very different conceptions of empowerment and professionalization than are permitted when unexamined assumptions about teachers and curriculum limit our vision. One conception of a professional and empowered relationship of teacher to curriculum is that of the teacher as active agent in curriculum deliberation, creation, critique, and change.

Teacher Agency

The term *agency* is used here to characterize relationships of teachers to curriculum that, like those described above, involve personal initiative and intellectual engagement. It is used as Arendt (1958) used the term *agent* to refer to one who initiates action. My use of agency here also draws on Greene's (1978a) use of the term *personal agency* as a form of autonomy that "carries with it a conviction of moral responsibility" and requires a continual wariness of "acquiescence and mindlessness" (p. 248). And, following Greene (1978b), agency requires initiating action that is "conscious, interested, committed" (p. 26) and remaining ever "conscious of mulitple possibilities" (p. 30). Agency involves action that is deeply tied to the person (Greene, 1978a, 1978b), and thus reveals or discloses the character of the agent (Arendt, 1958). Finally, agency involves engagement with others, for being an agent of action, according to Arendt, "is never possible in isolation" but only "in constant contact with the web of the acts and words of other(s)" (p. 188).

Teacher agency in curriculum matters involves initiating the creation or critique of curriculum, an awareness of alternatives to established curriculum practices, the autonomy to make informed curriculum choices, an investment of self, and ongoing interaction with the others. Teacher agency is possible when teachers are engaged in the creation of curriculum or when teachers explore "curriculum potential" (Ben-Peretz, 1990) in received curricula. Teacher agency in curriculum matters encompasses the activities traditionally labeled curriculum development, curriculum improvement, curriculum implementation, curriculum evaluation, and curriculum change, while challenging, and in some cases rendering meaningless, the traditional definitions of these terms. (See Snyder, Bolin, & Zumwalt, 1992, for example, for an analysis of alternative perspectives on curriculum implemetation.)

The phrase "teacher agency in curriculum matters" cannot be understood apart from the definitions of curriculum and teacher that it assumes. The term agency assumes not only a particular role for teachers that is at variance with prevailing assumptions of the teacher as technician or as implementor of others' ideas, but also a conception of curriculum not as a reified and easily generalizable commodity, but as an evolving, context-specific interaction between teacher, children, and content. Therefore, "teacher agency" not only

Figure 1.1 *Relationships between conceptions of curriculum and conceptions of teacher*

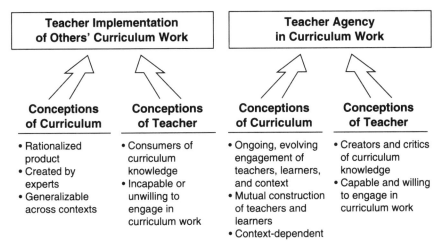

defines a relationship between teachers and curriculum, it also assumes particular definitions of curriculum and teacher. Figure 1.1 illustrates the interdependence of the meanings of these terms.

The teachers' curriculum work reported here reflects the interrelated assumptions about curriculum, teacher, and the relationship between them that characterize agency. Although the details of each teacher's curriculum work differ in numerous and significant ways, their conceptions of curriculum and the ways they conceived of themselves as teachers and their relationship to curriculum are consistent. In the following chapter, each teacher is introduced and her agency in classroom curriculum work is described.

2 The Teachers

Summit Grove Elementary School is the largest elementary school in the West Brook Public School System.* Located just outside a large eastern city, the school and its surrounding neighborhoods are characterized as suburban-urban. Quiet streets of row homes lie between bustling citylike business areas and sprawling suburban shopping centers. Once a traditional homogeneous white working-class neighborhood, the area surrounding the school has grown in recent years to include an ethnically mixed population working in service industries and the professions in the city. Now the children of recent immigrants from the Middle East, Greece, and Southeast Asia and of a very small number of Black American families attend Summit Grove with children whose families are long-time residents of the area.

Housing more than 600 kindergarten through fifth grade children and their teachers at the time of the study, Summit Grove's ever-increasing enrollment far exceeded its intended capacity. Large open-space classrooms designed to house three classes had been divided into separate spaces with shelving, movable chalkboards, folding partitions, or permanent walls when open education fell out of favor and increasing enrollment made it difficult to merge large classes for instruction. When the school district designated Summit Grove as the central site for ESL instruction, and transported all of the eligible students in the district to the school, every available space was called into service to house language teachers and support staff.

Crowded classrooms seemed to spill out into the hallways. Seated on floors or at desks outside their classroom doors, pairs and small groups of children collaborated on written work or prepared presentations. On the walls and ceilings around them hung lively displays of children's writing, paintings, drawings, diagrams, timelines, charts, and constructions. Walking through the halls, the feeling one had was not of crowdedness, however, but of purposeful bustle. Although endless lines of children proceeding to and from the playground, row after row of cafeteria tables overflowing with children, and countless clusters of teachers and their children gathered in the gym for spe-

---

*Throughout this book, all names of schools, teachers, and students are pseudonyms.

cial programs produced much noise and energetic movement, there was little of the friction or contentiousness found in many overenrolled schools. A sense of energy and common purpose prevailed.

This was attributable, in large part, to the stability and cohesion of the faculty. Few teachers had left the faculty and few new teachers had been hired since the school opened 15 years before. In that time, the teachers had developed a shared identity. They perceived themselves as open to, and knowledgeable about, curriculum innovations and also as responsive to the needs of all of the children. At the time of the study, some teachers were exploring classroom uses of computers and other technology, and the faculty as a whole was strengthening the language arts curriculum to meet the needs of the increasing number of children with developmental language delays and children for whom English was a second language.

The invitation to participate in a study of word processing and children's writing development was welcomed by the principal as an opportunity to support and extend the teachers' explorations of computers and focus on developing written language skills. According to the agreement with the researchers, three teachers—a kindergarten teacher, a second-grade teacher, and a fourth-grade teacher—were to be given at least two microcomputer systems and word processing software in the first year of the study. The researchers would instruct the teachers in the use of the hardware and software, and as part of the university's teacher education practicum program, place a university-student teaching assistant in each classroom two mornings a week during the fall semester. Each teacher was to be free to decide what word processing skills she would teach her children and how, when, and to whom she would teach these skills. Furthermore, each teacher would determine the ways in which she and her children would use this writing tool in their curriculum. In the following year, two additional teachers—one each from the first and third grades—were to join their colleagues and they too would receive hardware and software, training, and university-student teaching assistants. In exchange, each teacher would be asked to permit a member of the research team to observe and document her children writing with word processing and to document her own curriculum work. The principal invited one teacher from each of the designated grade levels to participate.

The group of teachers who responded to the principal's invitation was demographically representative in age, years of experience, and education of all of the teachers in the work force. Their ages ranged from 25 to over 40, and their years of teaching experience from 3 to more than 20, which with the exception of one very young teacher with 3 years of experience, was typical for all public school teachers (median age, 39; median years of experience, 14, Bureau of the Census, 1987). The teachers were representative in terms of professional education as well. Most had earned bachelor's degrees at state teachers colleges. One of the five teachers held two master's degrees, one was near completion of her graduate degree, and one was beginning graduate work (46.2% of the teaching force held master's degrees in 1986, Bureau of the Census, 1987).

It was not their representativeness as a group, but their uniqueness as individuals, however, that was their most salient characteristic for the purpose of this study. Each of the teachers joined the research project with different goals for herself and her children, and different perceptions of word processing as a skill to be learned and as a tool to be applied to other curriculum areas. Each teacher brought to her curriculum work her own interests, skills, past experiences, and current concerns about curriculum. The curriculum that each developed differed from the curricula developed by her colleagues in significant ways that went beyond the difference in the ages of the children they taught.

Barbara Gold, a first-grade teacher; Margaret Price, a second-grade teacher; Debby Perrone, a third-grade teacher; and Beverly Winston, a kindergarten teacher are introduced in the portraits that follow. One teacher asked not to be represented in this report of the study. (See the Appendix for a discussion of the methodological issues raised by honoring this request.) These portraits establish the unique character of each teacher's curriculum work, the way she conceived of her relationship to the curriculum, the role she took in curriculum change, and the personal and professional goals and beliefs that guided and shaped her work. Although these introductions are intentionally brief, merely foreshadowing the themes and patterns developed in the chapters that follow, they orient the reader to each teacher's perspectives on curriculum. It is through their perspectives that the contexts and processes of the teachers' curriculum work will be analyzed.

BARBARA GOLD:
INDIVIDUALIZING IN A CLIMATE OF STANDARDIZATION

Barbara Gold's first-grade class was located in one of the few self-contained classrooms at Summit Grove. Like Barbara herself, the class was characterized by its constant animation and warmth. Barbara and her children laughed and hugged easily.

The children's desks were arranged face-to-face in three short columns at one end of the room. The hand-lettered name cards taped to each child's desk revealed the multi-cultural character of Barbara's class. *Sung Ho, Christos, Joel, Marcus, Padmini, Alexandra, Heather, Huan, Melinda, Ho Sook,* and other names were printed in perfect two-inch letters on tagboard strips now worn from the children's repeatedly tracing the letters, surreptitiously decorating them with crayons and markers, and frequently removing them to pass to a classmate to be copied into a story-in-progress.

Surrounding the children's desks were shelves of learning games, and there were empty tables and a carpeted area on which to use them. One low shelf was tightly packed with children's literature; another held the children's art supplies. An easel with tempera paints and large pieces of newsprint stood beside the long low tables. Children who had completed their assigned tasks at their desks were free to use these areas of the room in groups of two or three. Relaxed movement and a constant hum of purposeful talk were frequently punctuated by quiet laughing and Barbara's quiet reminders to children or enthusiastic announcement of a child's triumph.

Barbara, a veteran teacher who had earned several advanced degrees in her more than 20 years of teaching, was respected by colleagues and members of the community for her skill in working with children with limited English proficiency or language delays. Consequently, each year her first grade classroom included a number of children whom the principal and other teachers felt would benefit from her special talents and the curriculum she had carefully constructed to respond to their needs. Her curriculum was grounded in her belief that a strong self-concept is a precondition for learning. She considered the failures experienced as a result of inappropriate curriculum to be significant threats to a child's self-concept and consequently to his or her learning. An ardent advocate for her children, Barbara described them as having experienced more failure than most and thus needing more to succeed. She wanted them to "feel good about themselves" and to feel that they were "part of" the literate population of the school. Barbara wanted them to feel independent and cheered their rebellion when someone tried to do for them what they now could do for themselves. She critiqued potential curriculum content and materials carefully against her belief that children's success as learners was related to their perceptions of their own capabilities. No practice that might threaten her children's self-concepts or cause them to question their own independence was tolerated.

Barbara's carefully constructed curriculum had been compatible with the school district's long-standing curriculum policy, which she described as a "laissez faire" approach in which teachers selected the curriculum goals and materials they deemed appropriate for their children. Just prior to the beginning of the research project, however, a school-district curriculum policy established a standardized curriculum for all children and teachers. It was Barbara's contention, however, that every class and every child is different and therefore that prescribed curricula were rarely right for her children. Acting on her conviction that the individuality of children and teachers must be respected, she confessed to making her "own rules" rather than following mandated curricula that she felt were "inappropriate."

At the time of the research project Barbara was most concerned about the mandated writing curriculum and the new reading series. For Barbara, two aspects of these curricula were the focus of a great deal of careful thought—the use of invented spelling for beginning writers and the practice of having first graders write independently in journals. The school district required that all children use invented spellings in their initial writing experiences, but Barbara felt her children were very aware that some spellings were right, that others were wrong, and that they were not yet able to produce correct spellings. Encouraging her children to use invented spellings meant putting them in situations where they would be producing writing that, in their eyes and in the eyes of older siblings and parents, was wrong, thereby risking blows to their self-esteem. Similarly, she felt that independent journal writing for her children, before they had sufficient skill to spell some words from memory and to generate reasonable spellings from their knowledge of phonics, would be an exercise in frustration and failure.

Barbara considered both issues carefully, discussed them with her colleagues, and questioned them again and again in her own mind. In her journal, she wrote:

> These children appear to be less secure and therefore more hindered when it comes to free writing. Unlike many in kindergarten who can use invented spelling freely or those in kindergarten who have a sense of letter-sound relationships, these kids "know" there is a right way to spell things. They also know they have no idea how to go about all this. My top group is just beginning to make letter/sound associations. My hope is that by January they may be ready for journals. I want writing to be a meaningful/fun experience. Also, self-esteem is a very important ingredient in my room. I want them to succeed and feel good about it regardless of whether they're writing a letter for an entire word, or a beginning and ending sound, or an entire word.

Rather than implement the new curriculum as prescribed, Barbara drew on her established reading, writing, and oral language curriculum based on a Language Experience Approach to literacy learning. Instead of requiring children to struggle to write alone, the class worked together to compose stories about shared experiences such as class trips, school events, and art projects. Their stories were recorded by Barbara on large chart paper or the chalk board. Reading groups composed stories together using repeated phrases and familiar words and these too were recorded by Barbara as the children looked on. Children also wrote at least once a week with Barbara or me at the word processors. At first they dictated their stories and watched them appear on the screen as adults typed their words. Soon dictation was replaced by collaborative writing in which adult and child shared the encoding and typing tasks. As the children's knowledge of speech sounds and letters grew, they cooperatively spelled out and typed their own words with the adults acting as coaches. As Barbara perceived that a child or groups of children were growing in confidence and in literacy skills, she encouraged them to write independently and to use invented spelling as one of their strategies for getting their ideas on paper.

The vignette that follows is reconstructed from my field notes as participant-observer in Barbara's class and transcriptions of audiotaped writing events. It depicts basic elements of the writing and word-processing curricula Barbara developed and the classroom culture in which she conducted this work.

Barbara has just returned the work each child completed the day before, commenting on a particular strength in each child's work as she distributes the folders. All count and recount the stars for good work that they have accumulated to see if they have reached the number that will earn them a small prize from Barbara's desk.

Barbara directs the children's attention to the sample worksheets displayed on the board in front of them. She explains, in a tone of voice that suggests something wonderful is about to happen, that today there will be four rather than three pieces of work, and the children cheer. As instructions are given for each piece, the children strike confident poses and announce to their neighbors, or occasionally to the entire class, that it will be "*sooo* easy." Barbara smiles at their bravado.

As the children set about their work, Barbara calls a group of the most advanced children to the reading table. Today they will be dictating a list of things that they like to do, using the formula sentence, "___ said, 'I like to ___.'" It will be recorded, and remain on the wall to be referred to, as a pattern for writing sentences independently and a source of correct spellings for frequently used words.

In the meantime, I read the note Barbara has left me on the computer. She says that today we will be bringing the last few children to the computer to dictate stories about themselves that she will print out and attach to the self-portraits they did in art class. When she is finished working with the group at the back table, she will join me at the other computer. I sort through the stack of children's drawings that remain, and find the one that belongs to Dawn, a child who is not now in Barbara's group at the back table and is not working with the ESL teacher. I take Dawn's portrait with me to her desk and invite her to join me at the computer to tell a story about herself.

After she types her name, carefully referring to the letters printed on her self-portrait and matching what she finds there to the keys in front of her, I ask her what she wants me to type about her picture of herself. I model my interactions after the ways I have seen Barbara work with the children. When Dawn says "playing," I tell her that I'll make a sentence out of that—Dawn is play-ing—and that she already has the first word, 'Dawn,' typed on the screen. I explain as I type, "I'm going to move that flashing light, that cursor. It tells us where the next word will be . . . 'is' . . . 'I' . . . 'S'" and I point to each letter on the screen as it appears. I read from the screen "'Dawn is'. . . . Now I'll make a space . . . and type 'playing'. Do you know what letter I should type first for 'playing?'" She says "no" then "P," and she finds it on the keyboard and types it. We continue in this fashion, completing three sentences.

Between us, Barbara and I finish taking each child's dictation. After school Barbara will assemble their book of self-portraits to add to the classroom library.

In this manner, multiple opportunities were provided for the children to learn word-processing and literacy skills in the context of their own writing tasks and in the company of supportive adults. Neither the daunting task of encoding one's ideas in print nor the very grown-up–looking task of operating a word-processing system posed a threat to the children's growing confidence in themselves as learners, readers, and writers. In fact, the successful completion of such challenging tasks bolstered their growing self-confidence. The children's satis-fied sighs when they completed full sentences or their insistence on making enough copies of what they had written to share with friends and family mem-bers were evidence of their conceptions of themselves as successful writers. All the while, the mandated reading books waited on the shelves and arrangements were made with a class of older children to provide each child in Barbara's class with a writing partner to collaboratively produce the required writing assignments to be submitted to the school district.

Barbara regarded all curriculum, even mandated curriculum, as open to critique and adaptation. She perceived her role in curriculum matters as one of action and agency. Curriculum was constructed out of the delicate inter-play of her goals, her beliefs about teaching and learning, and her assessment of her children's strengths and needs as they emerged. The curriculum she created was responsive and ever changing as she and her children learned from their work together. She was careful not to call attention to her curricu-lum work, however, and chose instead to proceed discreetly and to quietly resist the curriculum policies that constrained her.

MARGARET PRICE:
MAINTAINING OPTIMUM CONDITIONS FOR GROWTH

Margaret Price is an experienced second-grade teacher. Her small frame and quiet manner conceal the wealth of curriculum knowledge that she has accumulated in her nearly 20 years of teaching. Margaret's classroom revealed a great deal about her own interests—particularly gardening. Displays of gourds and squash, forced bulbs, or seed pods were found at the entrance to her classroom at all times of year and live plants filled the shelves she had added in the small windows.

Margaret's class was housed in a shared three-space classroom where teaching areas were separated by tall cupboards and movable bulletin boards. Although each area functioned as a self-contained classroom, noise from the adjoining spaces had to be taken into consideration. Consequently, Margaret and her colleagues carefully coordinated their schedules to assure that noisy activities in one space did not interfere with quiet activities in another. Margaret's space was exceptionally orderly and calm. Children worked individually, occasionally speaking to each other in hushed voices. Few children interrupted either Margaret's work with her reading groups or her large group activities. Margaret's expectations of the children were clear and consistent. The time Margaret invested in giving detailed instructions for work—telling children how the work was to be completed, in what order it was to be done, where materials were to be found, where completed work was to be placed—paid great dividends. In what she described as her "harmonious classroom atmosphere," her children, like her plants, grew steadily. With the quiet patience of a gardener, Margaret adapted to the shifting curriculum conditions under which she and her children worked.

Margaret's curriculum work was guided by the personal and academic goals she held for her children. Goals such as using capital letters at the beginnings of sentences and to denote proper nouns, and using correct punctuation at the ends of sentences, were cited along with her desire that her children achieve an "awareness of and joy in participating in the world around them," "respect and tolerance" for others, and "good working relationships." She did not expect children to meet her goals on the first or even the second attempt. She provided ample opportunities for children to see skills demonstrated and values modeled and to practice them with the assistance of an adult. When teaching children to edit their writing, for example, she worked with pairs of children so that she could edit one child's writing while the second observed; the first child then observed while the partner's work was edited so that each could "see it twice." She never seemed to expect too much from the children or to expect to see results too quickly. She did, however, slowly and almost imperceptibly raise her expectations as her children progressed toward her goals. It was this careful matching of her expectations to the needs of the children at a particular point in time that may have accounted for her children's success and the reputation Margaret had earned among her colleagues as a teacher who consistently enabled even the most difficult children to succeed.

Margaret's curriculum was as harmonious as her classroom routine and as carefully constructed and reconstructed as her expectations for her children. For example, the curriculum she developed around the study of colonial life integrated curriculum goals from language arts, science, and social studies in a field trip to a restored colonial site, and activities such as candle making, extracting inks and dyes from plants, and making colonial dolls with dried-apple heads. Individual activities and entire teaching units had been carefully crafted over years of refining and testing them against her accumulated knowledge of how children might be expected to respond.

During Margaret's two years of work with word processing, the school district adopted a new writing curriculum, a different basal reading series, and a new handwriting program. Each new curriculum represented a challenge to Margaret's well-established "harmonious classroom routine" and the interrelatedness of her existing curriculum. Much was lost. Activities carefully created to coordinate with particular stories in the basal reader, tested and refined over time, had to be abandoned, and new ones devised to match stories in the new reading series. Margaret and Barbara discussed the difficulties of managing the new reading series at a research meeting held early in the new school year.

> MARGARET: Next year will be easier. . . . Right now, it's hard . . . because we haven't used it before.
> BARBARA: In first grade we use reading in a content-oriented way. When you got to the goldfish story, you did the goldfish unit in science. [Now] everybody's kind of feeling their way and finding what is appropriate when.
> MARGARET: All of the writing that we did was related to the stories in the reader. . . . So it's really hard now.

In addition, the school district now specified the number of minutes of daily instruction required for some of the curriculum areas. The time Margaret needed to develop her elaborate study of colonial life was threatened by required time allotments in existing curriculum areas as well as added curriculum areas such as health and handwriting. She responded by tallying the time she spent teaching a science lesson that included a writing task for both the science and language arts totals, thereby protecting blocks of discretionary time to devote to the rich curriculum she had developed over the years. Margaret maintained this and similar forms of quiet resistance to each mandated curriculum change that threatened to disrupt her carefully crafted curriculum and "organized routine."

Word processing presented yet another addition to her curriculum and another potential disruption of her practice. Yet it offered something she valued. She saw in word processing a way of motivating children to write, as well as a way to relieve children of the burdensome tasks of erasing, copying, and recopying their work to eliminate errors. But just as with all the curriculum changes that had come before, word processing had to be absorbed into Margaret's "organized routine." In the case of word processing, the most critical considerations were her three-reading-group structure and the schedule Margaret had coordinated with two other teachers that required she be involved with reading groups throughout the language arts period. Because timing and her careful articulation of content required that she conduct three reading groups each morning, it was imperative that Margaret's children quickly acquire the ability to use word processing independently, or that she arrange to have another adult available to provide assistance while she worked with her reading groups.

Initially Margaret chose to delegate the instruction and supervision of word processing to the university student who was assigned to her classroom two days a week as a teaching assistant and a researcher who observed once a week. In the second year she chose instead to instruct the children herself, working several days a week with one reading group at a time on word processing skills. When she felt certain that the children she was working with were capable of using the hardware and software without assistance, they were sent to the computers during independent work times. She then began to prepare another reading group to use word processing.

Several forms of support were available to the children while using word processing independently. First, the writing tasks that Margaret assigned them were carefully structured. For example, children assigned to write their own retelling of a story they had read were told to take their reading books to the computers with them to remind them of details and as a reference for the spellings of words they were likely to need. Support in writing and word-processing skills was also provided by pairing children. When composing, two children were sent to the computers to collaborate on a writing task. When editing their writing, each child was sent to the computer with a partner so that the partner could read from the paper-and-pencil draft while the author typed in the corrections.

The following vignette, reconstructed from field notes and transcripts of research meetings, illustrates the careful structure and integration of Margaret's curriculum and the supports she provided her children so that they could proceed independently.

The top reading group has just finished their daily lesson with Margaret. As the children gather their belongings to go back to their desks, Margaret asks Susan and Gwen to stay behind. She tells them that they will be going to the computer to write about the yam experiment that they had started the day before. She asks them to remember what they did. They describe filling a jar with warm water and using sticks to suspend the yam in the water. Margaret reminds them that the "sticks" are called "toothpicks."

Margaret and the girls go to a computer, passing the terrarium with a chart above it listing the numbered steps that they had followed to make it. As the girls settle into their seats, Margaret reminds them that the return key moves the cursor to the next line and that the letters they type will appear wherever they see the flashing green cursor. She asks them how they will begin writing their list of steps to root a yam. Getting no reply, she suggests that they number the steps as they list them, then asks what they did first in the experiment.

Gwen says that they got a jar. After providing quick reminders of how to produce a capital letter and make spaces between words, Margaret leaves the girls to continue on their own. The girls agree on each sentence they will type and then divide the typing word by word. Gwen types the word 'We' and makes a space, then Susan types 'got' and a space. Word by word they finish typing their first step, then they pause to consider what to write next. They continue working together in this fashion. When Gwen sees Susan struggling to locate a letter, she gently takes Susan's finger and moves it to the key she is seeking.

Nearby, Margaret occasionally glimpses up from her work with other children to monitor the girls' progress.

With the support of a quick review of an experience the girls had just shared, a reminder of the prior experience of composing a list of steps to make a terrarium, and a classmate to assist, the girls completed their five-step list, without Margaret's intervention, in 10 minutes. When Margaret described this event in a research meeting, she reported that she had been pleased. Responding with her characteristic expression of quiet satisfaction in her children's growth, she remarked that they had done "very well" in a tone that suggested that she had expected all along that they would.

By exercising quiet control over her curriculum in the face of external curriculum requirements, Margaret was able to maintain the conditions of order, calm, and continuity within which her children succeeded. In Margaret's carefully structured environment, children's learning proceeded in small predictable increments—the slow, steady growth that brought Margaret quiet satisfaction.

DEBBY PERRONE: MAKING A PLACE FOR HERSELF

Debby, the first new teacher to join the faculty of Summit Grove in over five years, referred to herself as "the new kid on the block." Young, insightful, and irrepressibly enthusiastic about her teaching, her thoughts flowed rapidly when she described her work. She was aware that although she had been employed as a long-term substitute teacher in the school district for two years, and had completed her first full year of teaching in the third grade, in the minds of many of her colleagues and in her own mind she was a "new teacher." Debby intended to change that perception. She had learned that in this school one gained the respect of colleagues by having and sharing skills and knowledge. Learning to use word processing in her teaching would provide her with what she regarded as "something special to share" that would allow her to establish herself as a respected faculty member.

The invitation to join the research project in its second year came at a propitious time for Debby. She had just completed a demanding year of learning the third-grade curriculum, particularly the soon-to-be-replaced third-grade basal reading program, and preparing for her summer wedding. Although there had been a computer available to her and her children were eager to use it, she had little energy or attention to devote to it. She explained in the initial interview:

> [The children] bugged me all [the time]. "Ms. Perrone, are we gonna get on the computer?" And I kept saying, "When I learn something, I'll teach you." I didn't know anything, and I felt so uncomfortable just, you know, being with third graders for the first time. I was weaving my way through the year right up to the end. . . . I didn't want to get myself too bogged down. Now I'm looking forward to doing as much with it as I possibly can.

However, this year, she explained, she had "energy" that she needed to "focus." The prospect of learning a new skill and enhancing her writing curriculum excited Debby, and she was eager to take on the challenge of exploring word processing and introducing it into her teaching.

Debby's classroom, like Margaret's, was located in a partitioned three-space room. Displays of her children's work under banners proclaiming their achievements shared the available wall space with posters that reminded the children of procedures for working independently. Debby characterized herself as a facilitator of learning rather than a teacher who is "center stage." She explained:

> I am a firm believer in the teacher not being the instructor in the classroom all the time. That's probably the basic premise of my teaching. . . . Teachers just need to create an environment where children can learn in any way they can and [the teacher can] just be a moderator.

She likened her teaching to counseling, which she was studying part-time in a master's degree program, in that supportive interactions among individuals

were central. Debby was rarely to be found in front of the whole group. She
was often on the floor with a group of children or conferring privately with
one child. If Debbie was leading a reading group, she was more likely to be
attending to the children at work throughout the room than exclusively to those
at her lesson because, as she said, she got much more satisfaction from seeing the children learn from each other than from seeing them learn by taking
instruction from her. Watching children work together on writing tasks brought
her particular pleasure. "Conferencing . . . is my favorite part. I love to watch
a lot of kids sitting around and reading their stories to one another."

Like Barbara and Margaret, Debby taught word-processing skills and
used word processing in ways that reflected her fundamental beliefs about
teaching and learning. Debby used word processing to support her emphasis
on sharing responsibility for learning with her children and to capitalize on
what she saw as the children's "inner eagerness" to teach as well as to learn.
Debby taught basic word-processing skills to those children who had slightly
more computer experience than the others and then created opportunities
for them to teach their less experienced partners. She commented on these
pairings in her journal in the second month of the year:

> Each couple is going to remain a couple until I feel that they can break
> away and work on their own—I feel strongly about the kids learning from
> one another. It is extremely effective.

After several months of formal peer teaching in pairs, followed by informal
peer coaching as children requested help, Debby surveyed the class about
their knowledge of word-processing procedures and was impressed with what
they had learned.

By her own admission, Debby loved to teach writing and loved to write
herself. She felt that in her first year teaching the third grade she just "didn't
do much" writing; it was, she said, "one of the things I was not ready to tackle,
and so I didn't." She explained that she had "let [her] two [grade-level] team
partners kind of guide me through what they had done in the past." But the
year Debby joined the research project, she said that she was "feeling a lot
more comfortable" teaching third grade and her writing curriculum grew and
flourished. Her children produced fat folders full of writing stimulated by
Debby's enthusiasm and creativity. Huddled together in the darkened classroom, she and her children told of the scariest things they had known, then
Debby sent them off to brainstorm and to draft scary stories. On another
occasion, the feel and smell and act of putting Band-Aids on imaginary wounds
stimulated spirited discussion among Debby and her children of the worst
injuries of their lives and provided the material for compelling collection of
stories. In addition to folders of their writings, accumulated over the course

of the year, the members of the class compiled books of collected writings and helped a kindergarten class publish a book that contained the younger children's dictated stories about their trip to the zoo; in addition, each child produced a book independently.

The school district's required writing curriculum seemed to Debby to impede rather than enhance her teaching of writing. In a discussion of the curriculum she was required to teach, she described the manual she was to follow to teach writing:

> We have an orange bound book—in our grade level the book is orange—called the Writing Process Approach, and it was a book that was developed by the language arts committee. It's just for the teacher, and all that's in there are 18 ways of prewriting—different ways to brainstorm. If there ARE 18 ways to brainstorm, they're in there! And [with a smile] they're the best ways, too! Don't try anything else!

She questioned not only the suggested topics for writing, which she found bland and trivial, but also the recommended practice of teaching the steps in the writing process prior to letting children compose real pieces.

> Last year I didn't do any story writing with them in the very beginning of the year because I didn't think they really knew what they were doing yet and I was going to teach them. This year I'm finding that they already know a lot of things and taking them through the process of writing—the prewriting and all—is really meaningless if they don't know that they're going to get a chance to use it. So you have to let them write right away.

Debby's stance of thoughtful critique in relation to the required writing curriculum characterizes agency in curriculum matters. Her way of thinking about curriculum was acquired, she explained, during the time she spent as a long-term substitute for the class of one of her colleagues.

> The kids [she] had [were] the top of the top. She was doing novels and fairy tales and folk tales, and she wasn't using the basal [program] at all. And that's all I had learned in my undergraduate training—how to open a manual and teach from it. So I continued with her program the best I could. I got a whole different feel for teaching from [a teacher's] own material as opposed to all the manuals.

With the knowledge that there were alternatives to following standardized curricula and the prepackaged plans in teachers' guides, and a taste of the success and satisfaction that was to be had, Debby, like Barbara and Margaret, met curriculum mandates with critique, questioning, and, when she deemed it necessary, resistance. And, like her colleagues, she gauged her resistance carefully, remaining within the bounds of what the system would tolerate.

The following vignette was constructed from researcher field notes and Debby's journal. It depicts events that occurred in April, when the children were working on their individual books. At this point in time, most of the children had completed several rounds of conferencing and revising their drafts with classmates; they were nearing the end of what had been a long and exciting project, and their enthusiasm had spread to the adjacent class-rooms. Debby took this opportunity to offer to share their collective exper-tise with the other third grade children and teachers. The vehicle for sharing word-processing skill was the production of a book authored by all of the children in the third grade to pass on to next year's third graders. The book would document "the best things about third graders and the best things about third grade."

> Children are writing, talking about their writing, and reading each other's writing throughout the room. Julie brings her paper-and-pencil draft to the computer. Although the task she has ostensibly set for herself is just to type in the text so that it can be printed out for binding, she is in fact replacing words and add-ing phrases as she types. When asked by a researcher who has been observ-ing her work to explain what she has done, Julie says that she simply "sees stuff" and changes it as she types. She returns to her work, concentrating on moving a sentence and combining it with another, which she accomplishes without help even though the researcher and Debby are easily available to assist her.
>
> As Julie is completing her typing and revision, Debby is preparing Caitlin to coach Beth, a third grader from another class, in basic word-processing skills. Debby reviews the assignment: to type the sentence stem 'The important thing about me is' followed by three phrases supplying detail, then 'but the most important thing about me is' and the appropriate conclusion. The students are then to insert the number of blank lines necessary to allow space for an illus-tration. Then they are to type the text for the following page: 'The important thing about third grade is' and repeat the structure established on the previous page. Debby also reviews Caitlin's role. She is to coach Beth without doing things for her. "Are your hands supposed to touch the keys? No, you show her and let her do everything else."
>
> Beth, with the delicate stroke of a key, begins by typing an incorrect let-ter. Caitlin reaches across from her position beside Beth to erase the character with the backarrow key. Debby, who remained nearby as the girls began their

work, remarks to Caitlin, "Uh-oh. I saw you reach for the keys. I know it's hard." Caitlin withdraws her hand and Beth begins again. When Beth looks up at the screen, she sees there is no space between 'The' and the letter that is to begin the next word. She erases the letter just as Caitlin had, then Caitlin shows her the space bar.

The girls continue working until lunch time, when Caitlin talks Beth through the procedure for saving the half-completed piece on a disk.

In a journal entry, in her third month of working with the computers, Debby summed up her thinking about her children and the word-processing curriculum she was creating for them: " I guess what I'm doing is providing anyone who comes to my room with an opportunity to teach themselves how to word process." And then in the spring she wrote: "I do feel like the kids have taught themselves and/or taught one another. . . . They're on their own! I JUST LOVE IT!" Debby had, in keeping with her belief in the power and importance of children teaching children, created word-processing and writing curricula that allowed her children to learn with and from each other, in their own classroom and in four other classes as well. Furthermore, she succeeded in distinguishing herself by achieving "something special," earned the attention and respect of many of her colleagues, and made great strides toward shedding the "new kid" image.

BEVERLY WINSTON: ADAPTING TO CHANGING EXPECTATIONS

For most of the 20 years or so that Bev Winston had taught kindergarten in the West Brook School District, the curriculum she created reflected her children's developmental needs for hands-on activity and her own delight in music, art, poetry, and fairy tales. But, symbolic of the ways in which the mandated curriculum was encroaching on the time she and her children could devote to these activities, were the clusters of tables for the required paper-and-pencil work that nearly filled the area near the chalk board, pushing the piano, easel, blocks, area for dramatic play, and manipulatives to the perimeter. Singing, talking, making, sharing, and enjoying poetry and stories, once central to Bev's curriculum, now took place only in peripheral times and spaces.

When Bev joined the research project in its first year, the school district had just announced that writing would be taught in all grades. For Bev, this marked yet another in a series of rapidly changing curriculum expectations. The introduction of the required writing program followed the district's adoption of a formal mathematics program with a workbook for each child. In the following year, a handwriting program and a reading program with another set of workbooks were to be added. As the content of the kindergarten curriculum shifted from developmentally appropriate activity to "academic work" that "trickled-down" from the primary grades, Bev's relationship to the curriculum was altered as well. Whereas for most of her career she had devised and assessed her own curriculum, she was now losing the autonomy, agency, and confidence with which she had previously engaged in curriculum work. It was perhaps the loss of confidence that was most striking.

Although the district mandated that all kindergarten teachers should teach their children to write using the district's version of a process approach to writing, Bev found neither the school district's expectations nor the means by which she was required to meet them very clear. She had been told that her children were to write, but not how much or how well. She had been told they were to use invented spellings, but how would they come to do that? Looking back on this period Bev, speaking for all the kindergarten teachers, said, "We never really knew what to expect of it—you know, how do you get this going?" Bev's frustration was expressed by two questions she repeated in our informal discussions, interviews, and research meetings: "But how do I get them past [writing] their names?" and "Are we doing what we should be doing?" Bev, who for years had successfully created and recreated her own curriculum, rich in children's literature, poetry, art, and music, was now looking for "hows" and "shoulds." Looking back over her first year of teaching writing, she laughed and commented, "I guess maybe at that point I was looking for a rule for the game."

Bev might just as well have been referring to her work with word processing. As a participant in the research project, she was invited to use word processing to support her teaching of writing. But unlike her colleagues, each of whom had a writing curriculum in place, she was faced with simultaneously initiating work with writing and word processing. Just as she asked school-district curriculum experts for rules for teaching writing, she looked to the researchers for rules for teaching word processing. Because the researchers had no ready answers, and were in fact there to learn with her how word processing might come to be used by beginning writers, she was left without guidance in this endeavor as well.

The little guidance Bev received about teaching writing or word processing served as her starting point. When she was told in an in-service training meeting to tell her children to "write something" on pictures they drew, she did so and then circulated among them to see what happened. Similarly, in response to the researchers' interest in what her children might do with word processing, Bev sent the children to the computers during their free play time and watched them explore and experiment with the machines. Her observations led her to challenge some of the procedures for teaching writing that she was learning in district writing workshops and to question the wisdom of using word processing with such young children. She questioned the effects on the children of typing on a keyboard that showed only capital letters. Would this inhibit their learning of lower case letters? Was this the source of her difficulty in getting her children to use lowercase letters when they wrote with pencils and paper?

The vignette that follows provides a glimpse of Bev's engagement with both writing and word-processing curricula in the middle of her first year of work with them. At this point she was concerned that many of the children continued to produce only "garbage" or random numbers, strings of letters, and punctuation when they used word processing, and that when the full class "wrote" with paper and pencils at the beginning of each day, few of the children were producing more than several laboriously drawn letters.

> Two children have chosen to work at the computers during their free play time. While Bobby settles into the seat in front of the keyboard, Sara has already begun her characteristic attack on the keyboard. He takes no notice of her as she giggles to herself, talks to children in the housekeeping area nearby, and dances her fingers over the keys. She rarely looks up at the strings of letters, numerals, punctuation marks, and symbols that rapidly fill the screen. Bobby, however, begins by scrutinizing the work left on the screen by the child who used the computer before him. He then reaches for the backarrow key to clear it, letter by letter, before he begins.
>
> Without a word, Bobby types the following:
>
> ilovemydadmom.
>
> He pauses for the first time since beginning, shifts a bit in his chair, coughs, and when asked by the researcher if he can read what he has written, replies in the musing tone of someone who has just remembered something important, "Wait." Bobby then sets back to work without further reply. He continues typing slowly and deliberately with one rigidly extended forefinger:
>
> nmystacee
>
> He utters a casual, "Whoops!" upon discovering an error in the spelling of his sister's name. Using the backarrow key he erases both e's, but when trying to replace one 'e' he holds the key down too long and gets three of them instead of one. Seemingly untroubled by this, he erases all three e's, then types one 'e' with a rapid stroke, and then a 'y'. His work now reads:
>
> ilovemydadmomnstacey.
> [I love my dad, mom, and Stacey.]
>
> Working entirely with words he can spell from memory, he continues to list family member's names in one long uninterrupted string.

That evening, Bev calls me on the telephone to reschedule next week's research observation around an unexpected assembly. With that taken care of, she begins excitedly to tell me about John. John had seen the news coverage of the shuttle disaster just before coming to the afternoon kindergarten session. He was fairly bursting with the story when he arrived at school and drew an elaborate picture of the explosion. Bev asked if he would like to write something about his picture at the computer while the others did the same at their tables. He produced—using his own invented spelling—the words 'space shuttle blowed up' and Bev hung them with his picture on the back wall of the classroom.

John's success prompts her to recall an event in the morning session. Micky, one of the most adept at representing words with the letters he "heard" in them, had asked her to type a story he "had in his head." It was an elaborate and wonderful story, more satisfying to both of them when recorded in this way than with the few painfully written letters that Micky had produced on his own with his invented spellings. It led Bev to question a decision she made early in the year when, because of the children's apparent lack of interest, she stopped using word processing to record the full-class dictation of the day's news at the beginning of each class day. "Maybe," she muses, "we gave up dictation too soon. Maybe we should be doing it with one child at a time. . . ."

Thoughts such as these marked the beginnings of Bev's return to a more active relationship to the curriculum. Posing questions, and looking to her children and her own practice for answers, marked a shift from her earlier search for someone else's rules to guide her work with writing and word processing. By the end of the first year of her work with the new curricula, Bev had tried a wide range of instructional approaches and writing tasks. Taking her cues from her children, she selected what appeared to be the most promising practices.

Bev's confidence and agency returned together. She began to defend her own practices and to articulate them to others. Once hesitant to have her children take home papers with invented spellings on them because she was concerned about parents' reactions, she began coaching her children as to how to explain to their parents what they had done. In a conversation recorded in field notes she remarked that in the past she would not have done "things like this," but that now she went so far as to instruct her parent aides on how to move children from dictating their stories to inventing their own spellings to record their stories. Near the end of Bev's second year of work with word processing, she felt confident enough in her curriculum to be a co-presenter of her strategies for using word processing and our research findings at a regional professional meeting of early childhood educators.

Bev began her work with word processing at a time when her well-established curriculum, built on her strengths and guided by her conviction that kindergarten should open children to the joys of learning, was being replaced by mandated curricula based on expectations that she found neither clear nor convincing. She reacted to these curricula and to her work with word processing by seeking rules and procedures to follow. Over time, and with great expenditures of energy and effort, Bev regained her earlier confidence and agency in her curriculum work.

SUMMARY

Striking differences are apparent in the work of these four teachers. Although some variation can be attributed to the different ages and abilities of their children, the most interesting differences between these teachers have to do with the goals, beliefs, existing practices, and concerns that guided and shaped their work with word processing. Barbara saw in word processing a tool with which her children could achieve the success in writing that they might otherwise miss, Margaret saw its potential for relieving her children of the tedium of recopying edited writing, Debby saw in word processing the opportunity to gain acceptance as a faculty member and as yet another arena in which children could teach children, and Bev regarded it cautiously as she assessed its potential for young children.

Equally striking are the similarities in the outcomes of their work. Although Barbara, Margaret, Debby, and Bev taught different word-processing skills, worked within different classroom cultures, were guided by different values and beliefs, used different instructional methods, and applied word processing to different writing tasks, the results they achieved were uniformly successful in four important ways:

1. Each teacher developed a word processing curriculum that effectively prepared her children to be confident users of the technology.
2. Each devised writing tasks and contexts that permitted her children to use word processing independently, with a minimum of teacher attention.
3. Each confronted assumptions about children, teaching, or learning and reassessed their validity in her own teaching.
4. Each teacher's enthusiasm and children's success prompted same grade-level colleagues to begin to explore word processing in their own teaching.

Each of these achievements deserves further exploration. The first, and most important to this study, was the effectiveness of the curriculum that each teacher created in the context of her own classroom. Without the benefit of teachers' guides, prepared materials, and mandated standards and tests of achievement, each teacher selected her own content and designed her own methods and materials for introducing word-processing skills to her children and assessing her own effectiveness. Each teacher decided what skills she would teach, when and how she would introduce the skills, and to whom she would teach them. Each designed lessons, activities, and materials to meet the needs of her particular children, as well as to fit the requirements of her own ongoing curriculum. Some teachers taught directed lessons, some taught informal, on-the-spot lessons. Some instructed the full class together, some taught small groups of children, and some trained parents or other children to teach individual children. Each teacher engaged in ongoing evaluation of the effectiveness of her curriculum. Lessons, activities, materials, and procedures that were judged effective remained in use only as long as they were effective; those deemed unsuccessful were revised or abandoned.

The second similar outcome of the teachers' work was that the children in each teacher's classroom used word processing competently and confidently, and the uses they made of word processing in their writing were extensive and varied. Documentation of the children's word-processing skills and writing development is provided in great detail in Cochran-Smith, Kahn, and Paris (1990) and Cochran-Smith, Paris, and Kahn (1991). It is sufficient here to point out that with very few exceptions, all of the children in each classroom learned to manage the hardware and software quickly and easily and made use of word processing within the limits of their writing skills and the writing tasks assigned. The youngest children dictated stories to be typed, shared the tasks of typing and spelling with an adult, composed their own stories using invented spellings, or collaboratively composed and typed stories, reports, or poems with a peer. The older children composed, edited, revised, and published their work on the word processor to the extent that their teachers emphasized these parts of the writing process. These children also tutored their peers and the younger children in word processing. Individual and class books were published, and prize-winning essays were composed on the computer.

Third, in the process of creating, evaluating, and elaborating or discarding methods of teaching word-processing skills and applications of word processing in their curricula, the teachers confronted some of their basic assumptions about children, teaching, and learning. Some of the questions raised and issues explored included the role of peers in children's learning, young children's ability to revise their writing, children's capacity for independent problem solving, the role of play in learning, and the value of full-group instruction in teaching writing. Some of the prevailing assumptions about these issues were challenged and others were confirmed, leading to the kind of professional learning described by Greene (1978) and documented by Bussis and colleagues (1977) in their study of teachers' explorations of alternative teaching methods.

Finally, colleagues of the teachers participating in the research project expressed interest in incorporating word processing into their own curricula. Among these colleagues were teachers who had objected to using computers in their classrooms and teachers who were resisting the school district's imposition of other curriculum changes. Over time they saw the children's writing displayed in classrooms and hallways, observed the project teachers work with word processing in their classrooms, and talked with them informally. In a slow, evolutionary process, which the principal referred to as "adding word processing naturally" and "inservicing ourselves," word-processing use spread to nearly half of the faculty, including teachers at all grade levels.

In addition to similar outcomes, a second similarity is also significant. All four of the teachers, although they differed in years of experience in teaching in general and in work with their existing curriculum in particular, took positions of active agency in relation to the curriculum—both to the curriculum they created themselves and to the mandatory curriculum they received from the school district. The character of their agency differed only in timing and in degree.

Barbara and Margaret, veteran teachers who were confident and comfortable in the curricula they had carefully shaped over time, responded with quiet resistance to the increasing rationalization and standardization of the curriculum they were required to teach and the decreasing opportunities to exercise their own discretion in curriculum matters. Neither of the teachers called attention to her work and neither allowed mandated curriculum to replace her own.

Debby, the newcomer, had spent the year prior to her work with word processing getting to know the required third-grade curriculum and not straying far from the expectations of the administration or the established practices of her grade-level team. But once she became knowledgeable about what was expected of her, she felt free to critique those expectations. The year she joined the research project was one of energetic curriculum making for Debby as she tested her growing knowledge and skill.

Bev, although a veteran who had previously exercised great control over her own curriculum, began her work with word processing in the least empowered relationship to curriculum. Having had her own well-developed curriculum replaced by one that was radically different in content and intent deprived her of the familiar and well-established base on which her colleagues conducted their work. Her initial response was to determine the rules and the standards with which she was expected to comply and follow them with little question. But, like Debby, once the expectations were clear to her she moved into a more active and empowered role in relation to the curriculum. She raised important questions and tested content and method against her prior knowledge and observations of her children. In time, Bev acted again as an active agent in relation to the curriculum.

As we turn to consideration of the contexts and processes of the teachers' curriculum work, it is important to remember that the purpose of this close examination of four suburban public elementary school teachers as they created and integrated word-processing curricula in their classrooms is neither to describe nor to predict the experiences of others. The value of this examination lies instead in the framework it provides, derived from the teachers' experiences and perceptions, for understanding teacher agency in curriculum matters. As knowledge of particular events contributes to the understanding of others (Eisner, 1981; Erickson, 1986), understanding the four teachers' particular experiences sheds light on work of other teachers and informs the efforts of those who would support them in their agency in curriculum work.

Part II
CONTEXTS

The significance of context in teachers' curriculum work has been established in the literature for both curriculum innovation and the introduction of computers and word processing in classrooms. This literature, although diverse in its theoretical perspectives, methodologies, and settings, as well as in the nature of the curriculum changes it documents, argues that context both influences and is influenced by teachers' curriculum work.

Sarason (1971) describes the "complicated embeddedness" (p. 11) of teaching and learning in the interests, histories, and established practices of multiple constituencies within and outside of the school. This complex context of schooling has been conceived of not as one uniform context but as many nested and interacting layers of context (Cochran-Smith, 1984; Cochran-Smith & Lytle, 1988; Erickson, 1986; Green, 1983; Heath, 1982; Ogbu, 1981). In these conceptions, teaching and learning are located within, at the minimum, the embedded contexts of classroom, school, and school district, with each contributing its own influences on and responses to teachers' curriculum work.

The classroom context has been characterized in the literature as a conservative influence on teachers' curriculum work. Cuban (1984), for example, documents the power of stable classroom practices to defeat or significantly alter proposed curriculum innovation. Leiberman and Miller (1984) describe the ongoing nature of classroom work, which requires that teachers keep their classes functioning while attempting to implement new curriculum practices. Similarly, Doyle (1979, 1983; Doyle & Ponder, 1977) calls attention to the impact of "classroom ecology" on teachers' decisions when they are faced with imposed curriculum change and characterizes these curriculum decisions as adaptive responses to the demands of the classroom context.

Structural features of the school context, such as team teaching arrangements and extensive record-keeping responsibilities, have been also associated with the manner and extent to which teachers engage in curriculum work. Gitlin (1983) found teachers' curriculum work within these

41

particular structural constraints to be dominated by the need to schedule, organize, and execute curriculum, leaving no time to engage in analysis and conceptualization of curriculum. The nature of interaction among school staff has been related to teachers' curriculum work as well (Connell, 1985; Little, 1982). In school contexts in which the norms of colleagiality prevailed, Little (1982) found that teachers collaborated in setting curriculum goals, producing curriculum materials, and evaluating curriculum.

The influence of the school district context on teachers' curriculum work has been documented in studies of large-scale curricular change (such as Berman & McLaughlin, 1978, and Gross, Gianquinta, & Bernstein, 1971). The attitudes of administrators toward the curricular change; the availability of support staff, money, and time for teachers during the change period; and the presence of strong and supportive relationships among district staff were associated with successful implementation and institutionalization of curriculum innovations (Berman & McLaughlin, 1978).

Although it could be argued that all teachers' curriculum work is affected to some degree by the contexts in which they conduct that work, it cannot be assumed that the nature of that influence is uniform across settings. Each classroom, school, and school district context is unique and the differences between them are non-trivial (Cochran-Smith & Lytle, 1993; Feiman-Nemser & Floden, 1986; Little, 1982). Therefore, efforts to understand teachers' work with curriculum—either curriculum they create and critique or curriculum that is created and mandated by others—must take into account the specific contexts in which that work is done and the nature of the relationship between context and teachers' curriculum work. Studies of the introduction of computer technology into curriculum frame context, in some cases, as a dependent variable altered by the introduction of computers into curriculum (Bruce, Michaels, & Watson-Gegeo, 1985; Dickinson, 1986) and, in other cases, as an independent variable that shapes computer use in the curriculum (Amarel, 1983; Cuban, 1986; Hawkins & Sheingold, 1986; Michaels & Bruce, 1989; Olson, 1986, 1988; Sheingold, Hawkins, & Char, 1984). Michaels and Bruce's (1989) work is representative of the second and somewhat more widely held position. In the final report on their study of computer use in two sixth-grade classrooms, they concluded that "the result of using an innovation was as much a function of the existing classroom culture as of the innovation itself" (p. 43).

Yet it has been argued elsewhere (Cochran-Smith, Paris, & Kahn, 1991) that linear conceptions of the relationship between context and teachers' curriculum work do not adequately describe or explain teachers' curriculum work. The relationships between classroom contexts and teachers' work with curriculum are more appropriately described as interdependent and compounded over time.

> Like the bank account in which yesterday's interest becomes part of today's principal when interest is calculated, word processing use that altered the classroom culture at one point in time became part of that culture which then shaped later uses of word processing. (pp. 69-70)

The relationships between context and teachers' curriculum work, then, are neither unidirectional or static, but interactive and evolving over time. Consequently, context cannot merely be documented as a precursor or backdrop to curriculum work, but must be treated as an integral and changing component of teachers' curriculum work.

Finally, the effects of context on curriculum and the effects of curriculum on context have been found to be mediated by teachers' perceptions of contexts and curriculum (Cochran-Smith, Paris, & Kahn, 1991; Feiman-Nemser & Floden, 1986; Olson, 1980). For example, teachers' assessments of what is possible (Doyle & Ponder, 1977) in a particular context define the parameters within which they make curriculum decisions. It is therefore necessary to consider the nature of context and its influence from the perspectives of the teachers themselves.

The aforementioned literature establishes the theoretical and methodological rationale for studying teachers' curriculum work in its contexts and offers ways of understanding the nature of the interaction between context and teachers' curriculum work. It also provides a background against which to address the central questions of Part II: What, from the perspectives of teachers actively engaged in the creation and critique of curriculum, are the most salient features of their contexts? And, what is the nature of the relationship between context and teacher agency in curriculum matters?

3 Contexts of Curriculum Work: School District, School, and Research Project

The impact of three contexts—the school district, the school, and the research project—was evident in the data on each teacher. The influences of these contexts were myriad and complex. Two categories of influences were consistently associated with the teachers' curriculum work. The first was the past and present influence of policies and practices within each context. Routine ways of conducting work in each context formed the foundation on which the teachers built their new curriculum practices. Second, underlying the policies and practices of participants in each context was a dominant ideology characterized by shared values, goals, and assumptions. Colletti (1987) documents ways in which ideology "penetrates" the work of teachers and how teachers negotiate the dialectical relationship that exists between the many layers of beliefs of their administrators, colleagues, parents, and children. For the teachers in this study, it was not only these negotiations, but also the teachers' assessments of these ideologies and their responses to the necessity of negotiation that influenced their work.

Each teacher's classroom context, then, was located within the embedded and interacting contexts of the research project, the school, and school district. The policies and practices in each context influenced and were influenced by those in other contexts. Each context reached back into the histories of participants and organizations, creating a dynamic system in interaction with itself over time. Finally, each layer of context reached down into the underlying assumptions and theories that characterized its organizational or personal system of meaning. Figure 3.1 summarizes the relationships between the contexts that were found to be salient in the teachers' curriculum work.

Although the school district, school, research project, and classrooms are considered separately for analysis, it must be remembered that none of these alone fully describes or explains the teachers' curriculum work. Attention to only one context or one point in time provides only limited understanding. Consideration of the multiple contexts and their historical and ideological roots brings forward for examination not only the origins, but also the accumulated

Figure 3.1 *Relationships of histories, ideologies, and practices in classrooms, research project, school, and school district*

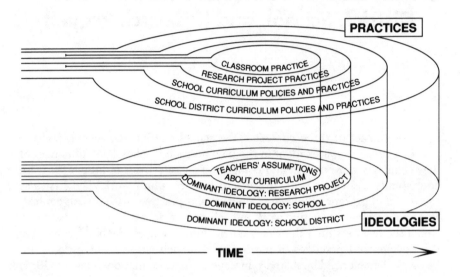

meanings of the ongoing policies and practices that teachers must negotiate when making curriculum decisions. Taken together, these multiple embedded contexts provide a deep and sound base on which to build understanding and support of teacher agency in curriculum work.

THE SCHOOL DISTRICT AS CONTEXT

Two categories of policy and practice and two aspects of the dominant ideology of the school district were identified as significantly related to the teachers' curriculum work and to their perceptions of their relationship to curriculum. The significant policies and practices included the systemwide movement toward a standardized curriculum and the associated means of preparing teachers to implement the mandated curriculum changes. The salient aspects of the dominant ideology were assumptions about the nature of curriculum and about the role of teachers in relation to curriculum. These curriculum policies and practices—past and present—and the ideologies underlying them guided and constrained the teachers' work with writing and word processing.

School District Policies and Practices

Much activity and spirited discussion surrounded the school district's new curriculum policies. Of particular concern to the teachers was the revision of curriculum to fit a predetermined standard.

Curriculum standardization. In 1985 when the study began, national attention to the perceived failures of schools had made accountability a central concern of school administrators. Like many others, this school district was engaged in a major program of curriculum revision and standardization in order to assure its constituents that the instruction it provided was of uniform and predictable quality. Prior to this time, individual teachers had selected their own teaching materials, and to some extent, their own curriculum topics. Margaret explained,

> For the first 10 to 12 years that I taught here, there were no curriculum guides. You know, there was nothing. I could pick three reading series. It had always been like that.

Under the school district's new curriculum policy, however, the varied and individualized curricula that teachers had offered their students were being replaced by a common curriculum for all teachers and all children. Margaret continued,

> When the district started organizing and making things the same across the board, things changed an awful lot and there's been a lot of pressure.

New central office administrators had introduced their comprehensive plan for curriculum review and standardization five years before the teachers began their work with word processing. In general outline, their curriculum revision strategy matched the eight-stage Curriculum Planning Model (Stellar, 1983) that was in wide use. Each year, one or more subject areas was brought to a committee of teachers and administrators for study. Over the course of the next two to three years, the existing curriculum was evaluated and alternatives were studied, then one curriculum was selected, piloted, implemented, and evaluated. In any year one or more subject areas were under review, others were at the point of selection and piloting, and still others were newly mandated.

The work of reviewing and replacing each curriculum area was conducted by committees made up of teacher-representatives from each grade level and school. Each committee was chaired by the curriculum supervisor assigned to the content area under review. The criteria against which existing and new curricula were to be judged by the committee were developed by the director of curriculum. The curricula selected for districtwide use were, for the most part, prescriptive programs accompanied by packaged materials, explicit instructions, and often prescribed time allotments, which served the school district's goal of standardizing teaching and learning across the district. During the period of the study, a single basal reading series was selected to replace the materials teachers had previously used, a uniform handwriting program was installed, and programs for teaching writing and health were added.

Two specific decisions made by the school-district administration during the course of the curriculum standardization process directly influenced teachers' work with word processing. First, the school district administration decided, after much deliberation, not to mandate a standardized computer curriculum. It continued, however, to require computer use in what the principal described as "a quiet, backhanded way." Computer use was encouraged and schools that used computers were looked upon favorably. But in the absence of district guidelines that specified the nature of computer use or of achievement goals that the children were to meet, teachers in the district continued to use computers in ways they found most appropriate or chose not to use them at all.

The teachers in the research project were therefore relatively free to create their own word processing curricula without the constraints of required content or methodologies, suggested assignments, timetables to meet, or minimum competencies to achieve. Debby described the teachers' work with word processing in the absence of a required curriculum:

> What we're learning is invaluable. . . . We're not sitting up there saying to the kids, "Well, no, you can't do it that way. I wish I could let you do it that way, but that's not the way [we're] doing it." I never have to say that to them. [I say,] "Sure you can try that. Go ahead!" and "Let me know what happens after you try it!"

Without the guidance or constraint of a standardized computer curriculum, the curricula the teachers created were responsive to the needs, interests, and influence of their children, and teachers as well as children were learners.

Second, the school district adopted a "process approach" to teaching writing. In the elementary schools, the model selected included a five-step procedure of brainstorming and prewriting, drafting, revising, editing, and publishing or otherwise sharing their writing with an audience. Children were encouraged to draft freely, focusing on content rather than correctness of form.

In the earliest grades, this included encouraging children to invent their own spellings. The presence of a mandated writing curriculum established parameters within which the teachers used word processing. The prescribed method of teaching writing, and the three assigned writing projects at each grade level, influenced but did not wholly determine the teachers' choices of the word-processing tasks and skills they taught their children.

When the study began, the process of adopting and adapting to the new standardized curricula engaged much of the energy and concern of the teachers and administrators in the school district. Teachers reported feeling that the school district's emphasis on fostering each individual child's growth had been replaced by concern with providing standardized experiences for all children. One teacher explained:

> What happened? [The district's] philosophy when we did our elementary self-study, and every other thing I had ever seen published by the school district, speaks of individualization. . . . The move is definitely— among some, I'm not saying all—. . . toward regimentation. Everybody looking the same. Less emphasis on the individual child.

Furthermore, the teachers experienced the progressive rationalization of curriculum as a denial of their own individuality, and the mandate that their existing curriculum practices be replaced as a denouncement of their curriculum expertise. These points of conflict are examined further in Chapter 5.

Curriculum training practices. Implementing curricula created by someone other than the teacher and instituted to standardize teaching requires that uniform instruction be provided to the teachers involved. For each new curriculum introduced, formal instruction was provided to all of the teachers in the district. Training presentations or workshops were conducted by curriculum coordinators, teachers serving on curriculum committees, or outside experts representing publishers of purchased curriculum materials.

In the case of the new writing curriculum, all of the teachers were required to attend monthly workshops led by school district language arts coordinators and teachers who served on the language arts committee. Teachers were grouped for training by grade level and each grade level was split into two groups—one for teachers with no prior experience teaching writing, and one for those with "some" experience. No one was exempted from training; even those teachers with extensive experience teaching writing were required to learn the school district's particular curriculum materials and expectations. As with the policies of curriculum standardization, teachers perceived standardized training and uniform expectations as a denial of their individuality.

Dominant Ideology

Undergirding and expressed in these policies and practices were assumptions about curriculum, curriculum knowledge, and teachers' relationship to both that were sources of continuing conflict.

Curriculum. The school district's process of curriculum selection and implementation and the nature of the curricula chosen reflected the industrial metaphor for curriculum and teaching found in the curriculum planning model described by Stellar (1983) and much of the published instructional material available to school districts (Apple, 1986). Curriculum was assumed to be a rationalized, systematized, standardized product created by experts outside the classroom and delivered to teachers for implementation. Teachers therefore required training in order to use it, with only minor modification, until another was provided in its place. Furthermore, curriculum was assumed to be context-independent. Produced outside the site of its use, it was assumed to be equally effective for every user in all settings. This conception of curriculum as a product limited curriculum committees to the task of selecting or creating packaged curricula, and it also precluded the possibility of considering curriculum as a process negotiated and evolving in a particular context or of considering teachers as engaged daily in its creation and critique.

Curriculum knowledge. Curriculum knowledge, or the knowledge of what to teach and how to teach it, was assumed to be the province of curriculum experts. The fundamental curriculum questions of what knowledge to include, and who should have access to that knowledge, were asked and answered by someone other than the teacher. Questions of how knowledge would be organized, and when and at what pace it would be made available to students, were also most often determined by someone other than the teacher.

Curriculum knowledge was perceived to be rational knowledge that was created through logic and experimentation. Excluded from and denigrated by this conception of curriculum knowledge was the personal, practical knowledge (Connelly & Clandinin, 1988) that the individual teacher accumulates over time through observation, experience, reflection, and deliberation with colleagues.

Teachers' relationships to curriculum and curriculum knowledge. In the dominant conceptions of curriculum in the school district, teachers' relationships to curriculum and curriculum knowledge were conceived of as rational and predictable. This most common characterization of teachers and curriculum in school change literature portrays teachers as "rational adopters" (Doyle &

Ponder, 1977) who systematically follow prescribed practices, convinced by information provided to them that the mandated curriculum and methods are better than those in use.

Apple (1983) argues that conceptions of teachers' relationship to curriculum and curriculum knowledge that exclude teachers from the creation of curriculum, and permit them only limited participation in its selection (in this case, teacher representatives measuring packaged curricula against standards established by the director of curriculum), exert a form of "technical control" over teachers and their work. Furthermore, the more rationalized and predetermined the curriculum, the less professional judgment is required or permitted from the teacher (Gitlin, 1983), thereby "deskilling" teachers (Apple, 1983). The dominant conception of the teacher's role was therefore one of increasing disenfranchisement and diminishing skill.

The school district was at a point in its institutional history of major shifts in policy, practice, and guiding philosophy. These changes were experienced by the teachers as a move away from the encouragement of individuality in children and teachers and as a period of energetic activity around curriculum change and conflict over conceptions of teachers and curriculum. To understand more fully the teachers' perceptions of the limits placed on their ability to exercise their professional judgment, and what those limits communicated to them about their knowledge, expertise, and individuality, it is necessary to examine the past and ongoing curriculum practices and dominant ideology of the school in which they worked.

THE SCHOOL AS CONTEXT

New curriculum policies and the concommitant ideological shift in the school-district context were significant to the teachers not only because they represented such a radical departure from the past, but also because they differed so greatly from the ongoing practices and dominant ideology of their school. Whereas the school district's policies, practices, and ideology focused on curriculum rationalization and standardization and diminution of the teacher's role in relation to curriculum, the school context supported and granted status to teachers' curriculum initiatives and individuality. The school context was characterized by an ethos of respect for teachers' curriculum work and pride in the school's reputation of having a distinct and clearly identifiable curriculum philosophy. The four teachers and their principal attributed much of the school's distinct character to both its physical layout and the faculty's shared history.

The open-plan classrooms and grade-level teaming of teachers permitted and required regular communication among the teachers. Some who shared two- and three-space classrooms, like Margaret and Debby and their respective grade-level teams, formed ability groups with children from the entire space for language arts or math instruction. Some teachers planned large projects as teams and shared responsibility for preparing and teaching science, social studies, or health units to their combined classes. The principal provided common free periods for grade-level teams to meet regularly for planning and preparation. In these shared spaces and shared planning times teachers became familiar with each other's curriculum knowledge and skills in ways that often are not available to teachers in traditional-plan buildings. As they collaboratively formed and assigned children to homogeneous reading groups or jointly planned and taught social studies or science units, the teachers became aware of and valued the particular talents, interests, and experiences of their colleagues.

Although the physical plan of the building helped make such communications possible, it could not make them desirable or productive. It was, according to the teachers and their principal, the history that the staff and the principal shared that made them so successful. Many of the teachers had taught together in another building in the district prior to their move to the open-plan school. Few new teachers had joined the staff for several years prior to the study. The personal and professional relationships among staff members had long histories and were exceptionally strong. Bev described the bonds among the faculty members in terms of support and mutual caring:

> There is such a tremendous support system . . . they're really so supportive. It's amazing to come here and feel so terrific. There's always such a good feeling. . . . People like to be together here.

Special occasions in faculty members' lives were celebrated by faculty room parties. Times of personal or professional difficulty were marked by colleagues' care, concern, and assistance. Social gatherings of staff members outside of school were common, and some even vacationed together or shared homes.

Common history and close association contributed to a school ethos in which personal and professional individuality and curriculum expertise were nurtured and rewarded. Yet underlying and consistent with their emphasis on individuality was what Barbara and Debby perceived as the faculty's unanimity in their beliefs about teaching and learning. They explained:

> DEBBY: Most of the teachers in our school think along the same lines.
> BARBARA: We do. . . . The philosophy is the same. And I think that goes way back. [The faculty] has been very stable.

It was the shared beliefs of this faculty that set them apart from the other faculties in the school district. Just as personal individuality within the school was highly valued, the individuality of the school among others in the school district was valued as well. There was a great deal of shared pride in the school's reputation of being different in curriculum practice and values from the other schools in the school district. Teachers recounted the common experience of expressing a view in a curriculum committee meeting and finding that theirs was the one dissenting voice or differing view. Barbara described these experiences:

> At these committee meetings . . . we start to say things and, for some reason, I've found more than once that we are sort of the oddball of the elementary schools. . . . And we do it time after time, no matter what the committee is. [Our school] always comes up with the oddball!

As this discussion continued, Debby added:

> DEBBY: When you walk into a big meeting and you wear your [school] pin . . .
> BARBARA: You don't HAVE to wear it!
> DEBBY: Just in case they're not sure!
> BARBARA: Until you open your mouth!
> DEBBY: Just in case they're not sure, I've been wearing mine. I don't know, but, you know, it's a great school. I wouldn't be anywhere else.

The recognition they gained in the school district for the school's distinctive views on curriculum brought both collective and individual satisfaction.

It is important to emphasize, however, that the views of the school context put forward here represent the perceptions of the teachers in the research project and not necessarily the experiences or interpretations of other teachers in the school. It is, however, the teachers' perceptions of the school context, and the policies and shared beliefs the four teachers identified as salient, that are important here because it is their curriculum work we seek to understand.

School Practices and Policies

Two clusters of school-level practices proved significant to the teachers in their curriculum work. The first was the teachers' engagement in curriculum initiatives, and the second, was their practice of sharing curriculum expertise, referred to by the principal as "inservicing ourselves." These practices were significant not only as fundamental components of the context in which the teachers conducted their work, but as counterpoints to the school district's emerging policies of standardization and control of curriculum.

Curriculum initiative. The dramatic shift in the student population of the school was an occasion for the faculty to engage in collective curriculum work. Many of their children, both native English speakers and those who spoke little or no English, were found to be in need of more and different language experiences than the children who had attended the school in the recent past. The faculty decided to focus their collective energies on building their children's oral and written language skills. Full-school events such as week-long celebrations of writing and reading conducted by visiting children's authors, classroom events such as "Author's Teas" with public readings of books published by the children, and daily emphasis on discussion, oral presentation, writing, and reading were part of their collective effort to develop a strong oral and written language curriculum.

In addition to collective curriculum initiatives, the school had a history of supporting individual teachers' curriculum initiatives in their own class-rooms. For example, more than five years before the district's move to a process approach to teaching writing, several staff members sought instruc-tion in this approach and attended writing workshops conducted by Donald Graves, a leading proponent of the method. Some of the teachers then en-rolled in local writing workshops or graduate courses to learn more about the process approach; others continued to study on their own. With the encour-agement of their former principal, they implemented what they had learned. Similarly, several teachers explored computer use in their own classrooms several years before the district began systematically investing in computers and software. With assistance from the Home and School Association and a central office administrator, machines and software were purchased. These teachers and their colleagues experimented with the new technology and assessed the available software against their curriculum goals.

Support for individual and collective curriculum initiatives at the school-level, rooted in a history of curriculum initiative during a period of greater teacher discretion, was maintained in the face of curriculum standardization and control by the efforts of the current principal. By virtue of her adminis-trative role, the principal was bound to provide assurances to the central office administration that the teachers and children in the school were adhering to the mandated standardized curriculum. By virtue of her own belief in individual variation and teacher initiative in curriculum matters, the prin-cipal was equally bound to support her teachers in their individual curricu-lum work. And she did both with aplomb.

The principal interpreted the central office administration's curriculum mandates as outlines of goals to be met. Her interpretation permitted teach-ers the freedom to meet those goals in whatever way they, in their own pro-fessional judgment, believed best. If a teacher chose to teach reading from novels rather than using the required basal reading series or to teach English in the context of the children's writing rather than using the prescribed materials, the principal supported her. The principal explained that "all [the teachers] have to do is [show] me that they're following through" with the school district's curriculum goals. Where specific activities were required, she encouraged teachers to "quickly meet the district's requirements" and return to addressing what they had determined to be their children's most pressing needs. She felt no need, she continued, to prescribe what or how the teachers should teach or to "check up on them." The principal had faith, based on her extensive knowledge of each teacher's work, that they would make the best professional decisions.

Further, the principal supported individual curriculum initiative by providing encouragement of and opportunities for these individual efforts. Bev summed up what she believed characterized the principal's support of the teachers' curriculum work:

> I've never really had anybody come and say I couldn't do that. . . . That's the unique thing. . . . She'll never tell you "no." I've never known her to tell anybody "no."

The principal described her own policies with teachers who were exploring new content or methods:

> My philosophy to work with the teachers in this building has been that if they have an idea and they're willing to work . . . to give them opportunities to do so.

"Opportunities" in the case of teachers interested in using computers included supplying all of the equipment and personal support they would need to introduce computers into their programs. At the time the study began, there were computers, software, and supplies available to every grade-level team that had been purchased with money from the principal's discretionary fund and with money solicited by the principal from the Home and School Association. There were also colleagues available to coach and consult with interested teachers.

The principal stressed that the initiative for exploring computers in the curriculum came from the individual teachers themselves.

> None of this was [the result of] directives from my office. The fact was that if they wanted to explore computers, I made sure that they got the computer, and made sure, you know, that the paper was in.

She saw her role in curriculum matters as catalyst and supporter of teachers' curriculum initiatives. By exposing teachers to each others' ideas and expertise and making colleague and material support available, she nurtured individual teachers' curriculum development and professional growth.

"Inservicing ourselves." At a district inservice meeting, the principal listened to a presentation made to the assembled faculties of several elementary schools about the ways in which another school in the district had introduced word processing into their program. Upon hearing the number of inservice training hours that were required and what it cost to train each teacher, she explained to all in attendance how in her school word processing expertise was spreading among the faculty through the interest and efforts of enthusiastic teachers. The principal told them that interested faculty simply came to their more skilled colleagues for help. "At our school," she explained, "teachers inservice themselves."

As Debby learned early in her tenure at West Brook Elementary, informal sharing of expertise was a highly valued practice with a long history. For example, teachers who were proficient at using videotaping and playback equipment taught their colleagues to use the equipment and were available to help whenever a problem arose. Teachers who had learned how to bind children's books conducted in-house workshops in bookbinding. Time was scarce in the teaching day, and many teachers had commitments after school, but teachers shared information informally in the halls and in faculty rooms in response to their colleagues' interest and questions.

In the case of word processing, the principal supplemented such informal sharing by arranging for teachers to meet with a colleague who had considerable skill and experience instead of attending districtwide inservice meetings. When school district adminstrators discovered the teachers' absence, they insisted that all teachers attend districtwide inservice meetings. The principal then negotiated with the district for a number of inservice days each year to be designated for teachers to meet in their own schools. The following year she was able to schedule a full afternoon of inservice time for teachers in the research project to meet with others at their grade level to share what they had learned about teaching with word processing.

Dominant Ideology

Underlying a history at the school of close interpersonal relations, and curriculum policies and practices that encouraged curriculum initiative, were shared expectations and assumptions about school-level curriculum practices. These shared beliefs, referred to extensively in the teachers' journals, in interviews, and in research meetings, fell into three related categories. The first was the centrality of collegiality in curriculum work; the second, the sense of collectivity in curriculum matters; and the third, the importance of individuality in curriculum work.

Collegiality and curriculum. Pervading the teachers' talk about curriculum and curriculum work was their sense of themselves as colleagues. One measure of the centrality of collegiality in curriculum matters was the frequency with which the teachers spoke in terms of "we" rather than "I," and referred to themselves and others collectively as "the girls." Even when discussing curriculum work in their own classrooms, they frequently spoke in the plural:

> And you know, some of the things that we do with the writing and the computers . . .
> We decided which one we wanted to do.
> We found a way that really worked where we gave them these intense units and we really got the kids involved and we thought that it was much more effective.

The teachers' sense of colleagiality and their shared assumptions about how one behaved as a good colleague were inseparable from their conceptions of curriculum work.

Socially constructed definitions of the central concepts in a context reveal much about the dominant ethos or ideology in that context (Grace, 1978). In this case, the shared definition of *good colleague* shed light on the ways in which the teachers in this school context conceived of their role in curriculum matters. Taking others into account when planning curriculum and sharing curriculum materials and knowledge were two fundamental characteristics of a good colleague.

"Taking others into account" was demonstrated by the consideration the teachers gave their colleagues' needs and wishes when planning curriculum, a characteristic referred to by Little (1982) in her study of successful schools as "inclusivity." When teachers planned their curriculum, there was an overriding concern about the impact of their decisions on their colleagues—a critical concern in a setting in which up to three teachers shared the same open-space classroom. An activity that would generate noise and motion would have to be planned when teammates were not doing work that required quiet. A lesson that was to be taught to two or three combined classes could not be extended, delayed, or rescheduled by one teacher without considering the impact of such a change on the other teachers.

Concern for colleagues significantly influenced the teachers' decisions about how they would use word processing in their curriculum. For example, questions were raised at an early research meeting about the possible effects on colleagues' relationships with the children and their parents of one class in the grade-level team having significantly more access to word processing than the others. Would parents argue that they wanted the same experiences for their children? Would children complain to their teachers that they wanted what the others had? Also, when the teachers met to plan their initial work with word processing in their classrooms, they expressed concern that the noise generated by the printers would disturb their teammates and that they would therefore have to limit the use of the printers to times when the noise would not cause a disturbance. Their concern was so great that a researcher constructed padded covers for the printers to absorb some of the noise. Only when the teachers were confident that printer noise—even without the covers—was not disturbing their colleagues did they consider a wider range of times for and uses of word processing.

In addition to taking colleagues into account in curriculum decisions, a good colleague in this context shared curriculum materials and knowledge. Teachers' personal materials as well as materials purchased by the school for individual classrooms, for grade levels, and for the entire staff were shared. It was not unusual for a teacher, in the middle of a lesson, to call across the room or across a partition or to send a child to another teacher to ask to borrow some material that could enhance or extend a particular discussion or demonstration. The expectation that materials were to be shared prevailed when the teachers participating in the research project received their computers and software. They immediately found ways for their colleagues and colleagues' children to share the technology. They produced ditto masters, letters to parents, party and field trip notifications, and film orders for their grade-level teams. Some coached their colleagues in the use of the hardware and software. Some, like Debby, planned joint writing projects with other classes so that more children could be introduced to word processing. In doing so, Debby shared not only access to equipment for word processing, but her knowledge of how to teach word processing to third graders and how to design writing assignments to take advantage of its capabilities.

Collectivity and curriculum. The centrality of collegiality in curriculum work was related to the teachers' shared view of curriculum as a collective rather than an individual enterprise The schoolwide focus on oral and written language development, for example, was based on a view of curriculum that extended beyond the individual classroom. Collectivity in curriculum planning was most marked, however, in some grade-level teams. By virtue of the similarity of their tasks, required materials, shared planning times and, in some cases, shared classroom spaces, many of the teachers viewed curriculum work from a wide angle, encompassing their grade-level colleagues' work as well as their own.

The principal held a broad view of curriculum as well. Her criteria for a successful curriculum initiative are illustrative. Rather than base her assessment on the number of individual teachers who had implemented a particular innovation or on the uniformity of its application, she assessed success in terms of the experiences a child would have as he or she passed through the school. In the case of teachers' adoption of word processing, she was comfortable with the fact that not every teacher had adopted word processing and that those who had adopted it were using it to varying degrees and in a wide variety of ways.

> In second grade, all children get experience on the word processor. Some have *more* than others do, but that doesn't upset me.

Discussing each grade level in turn, the principal reflected on the ways in which teachers' uses of word processing varied.

> [One teacher in the team] has taken off with it. The other two aren't taking off, but the kids are still doing it and getting some experience with it.

> [One teacher was] finding a way that was natural for her to work with the kids at that age level. . . . Across the hall, the other two teachers . . . are less adventuresome. . . . But they *are doing some* word processing.

It was more important to her that somewhere "along the line" the children would have extensive and varied, although not identical, experiences with word processing and leave her school at the end of fifth grade proficient in word processing.

At the time of the research project, the principal was working to increase contact and exchange of experiences and concerns between teachers in all curriculum areas across as well as within grade-level teams. She was looking for opportunities for teachers to meet with those in the grade levels that preceded and followed their own. Her immediate goal was to increase articulation of children's experiences as they moved through the grades.

The growing sense of collectivity in curriculum work in this school context was evident, in nascent form, in some of the teachers' discussions in research meetings during the second year of the project. Concern was expressed, for example, about the continuity of experience for the children in project classrooms. Children who had been in project classrooms in the first year, but were assigned to classrooms without computers in the second year, were considered as possible classroom aides to the younger children so that they could continue to get word-processing experience. Children who had been assigned to project classrooms in the previous year were considered by their project teachers in the second year "computer experts" who could coach their less experienced peers. Questions were raised as well about other teachers' reactions to children who had had computer experience. Bev, who at the time attributed her kindergarten children's preference for printing capital letters to their exposure to capital letters on the computer keyboard, confessed:

> I wonder what I'm going to hear from the first grade teachers. These kids are writing in capital letters.

Others expressed concern that children entering a grade level in which none of the teachers had begun to use word processing would "bug" their teachers about their lack of access to word processing. Like their principal, the teachers expressed a cumulative view of curriculum that focused on children's experience with word processing across grade levels rather than their experiences within a single classroom.

There were, of course, teachers who did not plan curriculum with grade-level colleagues, teachers who shared materials and expertise less freely than others, and teachers who viewed curriculum as a more narrow, classroom-bound enterprise. But for the teachers whose work is documented here, the collegiality was a critical aspect of curriculum work, and curriculum was defined as a collective enterprise that extended beyond the individual classroom. Yet in and compatible with a school context that emphasized collegiality, individuality was highly prized and carefully protected.

Individuality and curriculum. The school district's history of laissez faire curriculum policies and the school's history of curriculum innovation and supportive relationships among teachers and principal contributed to the development of distinctive teaching styles in individual teachers. Individual variation among teachers in knowledge, skills, and interests was valued for what it contributed to the school community. Teachers were respected for their expertise and were expected, as good colleagues, to share their talents with others. Individual teachers were known and respected for a wide variety of talents and skills. A teacher who was particularly talented in storytelling was invited into her friend's classroom to tell stories. Another teacher enjoyed music and played piano very well; she led all the kindergarten classes in singing. Several teachers who had learned to use videotaping equipment were on call to assist others who wanted to use it, and they managed the scheduling and maintenance of the equipment as well. Another teacher was the school's computer expert and instructed all of the faculty in the basic use of the machinery. She reviewed software, recommended particular pieces to teachers, and was on call to assist with hardware or software problems. Teachers with skills that others sought taught their peers.

Individuality in teachers' knowledge and skill evoked admiration and respect in other teachers rather than envy or feelings of inadequacy. Debby described spending a day at a colleague's house when she first began to learn word processing.

She's the most non-threatening person you'd ever want to meet! . . . The perfect person to have my first lesson [with]. I really appreciated that because I didn't feel dumb. I could ask any stupid question.

The principal also expressed her appreciation of the curriculum skills and knowledge of individual teachers. When discussing the spread of word processing through the school, she described the value of having a skilled teacher available.

> You know, [she] is our resource person in the building. That, I think, is a very important factor. We need someone who has the knowledge, so that teachers can just say, "Hey, how do you ___?" . . . She does wonders for us.

The principal's strategies for encouraging each individual teacher's curriculum initiatives were not viewed by other teachers as preferential treatment. Her provision of meeting times for teachers to share skills with their colleagues, the opportunities that she made available to individual teachers to attend small workshops to explore curriculum topics of individual interest, and her support of teachers who chose not to follow the standardized curriculum as prescribed but to meet the goals in their own ways were seen neither as expressions of favoritism nor as implied deficits. As the principal pointed out,

> I mean, they're not going to feel threatened because the other people aren't attending this workshop or saying, "How come those people are doing something else when I could be doing that?" I mean, there might be some buildings where that happens.

Variations in teachers' curriculum knowledge and experience were valued and nurtured rather than hidden or struggled against.

In the context of the existing policies and practices and of the dominant ideology of the school, mandated school-district curriculum was treated as an outline of goals to be reached. Taking the requirements of the school-district curriculum into account, the teachers created their curricula. These curricula were shared constructions, encompassing not only the talents and interests of colleagues, but their material and scheduling needs as well. Curriculum knowledge was viewed not as externally discovered and delivered, but as created daily by teachers working in their own classrooms alone or with grade-level teammates. It was passed on from colleague to colleague through informal interactions as well as formal meetings within the teacher's grade-level or school. The teachers' role in relation to curriculum and curriculum knowledge was conceived of as an active one. Teachers were creators and critics of curriculum and teachers of their own colleagues. In relation to received curriculum, they were adaptors rather than adopters. Within a school district striving for standardization, the school's policies, practices, and underlying ideology encouraged teachers' individuality as creators of curriculum and agents in their own learning and the learning of their colleagues.

The research project constituted the third context within which the teachers conducted their work with word processing. Although smaller in scope and lacking the complex history of the school district and school contexts, it nonetheless contributed to the complex and often conflicting practices and ideologies that shaped the broader context of the teachers' curriculum work.

RESEARCH PROJECT AS CONTEXT

The Microcomputers and Writing Development Project, an ethnographic study in its theoretical framework, methodology, and guiding questions, assumed that teachers would be participants in rather than subjects of the study. The researchers were interested in learning from and with the teachers and their children about what part word processing would play in the work of beginning writers and their teachers. Consequently, the research design did not control conditions or subjects and did not isolate and manipulate variables. Instead, the teachers were asked to incorporate the use of word processing into their ongoing writing curricula and to allow the researchers to observe and document what transpired. The teachers, as holders of privileged knowledge of their context and their children, were looked to as contributors of significant observations and judgments during the collection and analysis of data.

The research practices designed to support the way the research was conducted were also intended to support the teachers' work with writing and word processing. The practices that evolved, however, often intruded on and constrained as well as facilitated the teachers' curriculum work.

Practices

Four practices—the provision of curriculum materials, weekly classroom observations, monthly meetings of teachers and researchers, and a week-long summer workshop to introduce teachers to the hardware, the software, and the research project—were the focus of much discussion among teachers and researchers. Researchers' field notes, interviews, and research meetings documented the ways in which these practices supported the teachers' active engagement with writing and word processing curricula or intruded upon or hindered that work.

Curriculum materials. There was a marked contrast between the curriculum materials supplied by the school district and the computers and word processing software provided by the research project. Whereas packaged, standardized curriculum materials prescribe content and often method, computers and word-processing software do so only in so far as they require instruction to be provided in their use. Beyond such initial instruction, the computer is considered a "flexible, interpretable device" (Sheingold, Hawkins, & Char, 1984) or a "Protean tool" (Papert, 1980). Unlike prescriptive curriculum materials, computers leave questions of content and aims to the teacher. Teachers can, by their choice of software, shape computer applications to match their own philosophies and goals.

Software selection determines, for example, not only the content to be addressed, but the means of instruction as well. "Tutor" software provides instruction and drills on discrete skills; "tool" software, such as word processing, data base, and spreadsheet software, provides the means by which tasks can be accomplished more easily; "tutee" software permits the student to "teach" or program the computer (Taylor, 1980). The researchers rejected software designed to teach and drill discrete writing skills, such as grammar and spelling, because it emphasizes mechanics over meaning. This emphasis is inconsistent with current research on the teaching of writing and with the beliefs and practices of the teachers and researchers. Word-processing software, on the other hand, supports the process of writing by managing some of the rudimentary mechanical tasks, such as correct formation of letters, left-to-right progression, spacing, and ease of correction, permitting students and teachers to concentrate on composing. Word processing does not determine the aims or the content of the teacher's or the student's work. The Bank Street Writer word-processing program was selected because the researchers considered it sophisticated enough to support a process writing curriculum and easy enough for the youngest children in the study to use. And because of its wide use in elementary schools at the time of the study, the program was also of potential interest to other educators.

Whereas the nature of the curriculum materials provided empowered teachers to make significant pedagogical decisions, the process of selecting these curriculum materials did not. Both hardware and software were acquired without consultation with the teachers. IBM, a major source of funding for the study, donated their own hardware. The choice of software, limited only by the availability of software that was compatible with the IBM computers, was determined by the researchers before their first meeting with the teachers. The teachers were not pleased with the complexity of the IBM keyboard or of the software's multiple menus, the complex procedures for printing and saving texts, and the cumbersome procedure for printing multiple copies. There was much discussion in the early meetings of teachers and researchers about the appropriateness of the researchers' choices. Although treated at the time by both researchers and teachers as hardware and software problems, in retrospect, the manner in which the decisions about the hardware and software had been made may have been an issue as well. Hardware and software ceased to be an issue when, on the teachers' initiative, teachers and researchers together began exploring the possibility of purchasing spell-checking software and assessing the appropriateness of various programs to teach keyboarding skills.

Weekly observations. Each teacher was observed weekly by one researcher. Each teacher-researcher pair negotiated and renegotiated two important features of the observations. The first was the scheduling of weekly observations to coincide with times that children would most likely be using word processing. The second was the establishment of a suitable role for the researcher to play in the classroom.

The intent of the weekly observations was to document the children's work with word processing when it occurred, but in no way to prompt work that would not have occurred otherwise. In actuality, however, if the teacher wanted the researcher to observe a particular word processing lesson or observe children working on a particular task, she was constrained to schedule it when the researcher was available. In addition, teachers felt obligated to have children doing word-processing work at the scheduled observation times, even when, in their best judgment, the time was not appropriate. For example, Margaret described the pressure she felt to begin using word processing far sooner in the school year than she had planned because an observation had been scheduled.

> It probably would have been better for the first month or so not having you come in. Then I could have started things, fiddled around, done what I felt like doing without a specific time. Like I knew Jessica [researcher] was coming at 10 o'clock on Tuesday mornings and [that we] had to do something at that time. That was it. It would have been better the first month not having someone coming until the routine had begun, and then you could know that every day at that time you ARE using the computer. It wouldn't make any difference if [the researcher] was coming or not.

The weekly observations, in effect, influenced the scheduling of word processing instruction and the nature of the tasks assigned.

The roles taken by the researchers influenced the teachers' work as well. Researcher roles varied across teacher-researcher pairs and within each pair over time. Researchers' roles included following the teachers' directions to instruct or assist children as they worked with word processing, observing without interacting with the children, observing specific children in response to a teacher's request for specific feedback about behavior or skills, or teaching a demonstration lesson. In Bev's and Barbara's classrooms, for example, I worked directly with the children at the computers, coaching and assisting, and, in some cases, instructing. In Margaret's classroom, another researcher initially instructed the children in word processing and writing, then as the children became more proficient, moved into the role of observer and occasional assistant. In Debby's classroom, the researcher was primarily an observer, although always available to assist when needed.

Teachers reported benefits from the weekly observations. Bev and Barbara, the teachers of the youngest children in the study, expressed their pleasure in having "another set of hands" available to assist. Bev's belief was, "If you're in here, you work!" Barbara expressed a similar sentiment in a note to the researcher about her plans for both of them to type the children's dictation at the computers: "I can't imagine 'wasting' you by allowing you to be a passive observer!" In the first year of her work with word processing, Margaret depended heavily on the help of the researcher and the university-student teaching assistant assigned to her classroom to provide word-processing instruction to individual children while she was occupied with her reading groups. "If I hadn't had [the teaching assistant] two days a week and had Jessica [the researcher] and used them to help out, I wouldn't have been able to do anything at all."

As the teachers and researchers grew more comfortable with each other, the teachers took greater control over the roles the researchers played in their classrooms and the scheduling of the weekly observations as well as the way in which they were conducted. As they did so, scheduling became more flexible, accommodating school assemblies, testing, field trips, school and university holidays, as well as the teachers' preferences to have or not to have the researcher present.

Research meetings. After-school research meetings were scheduled monthly in a teacher's classroom. The meetings were designed to provide teachers and researchers regular opportunities to share what they had done, observed, and thought about since the previous meeting and to discuss their hypotheses about what had transpired. Although teachers in this school had time to discuss their work with their grade-level colleagues in shared free periods or lunch times, they had few opportunities, if any, to talk with their colleagues in the research project who were from different grade levels. Consequently, the researchers planned the monthly meetings as opportunities both to advance their own understanding and to provide the teachers with a way of sharing their experiences and learning as the researchers were doing, from their colleagues.

Although time was primarily devoted to recounting the highlights of the month's work, periodically, significant questions of practice were raised. For example, in the following excerpt from the transcript of a research meeting, Barbara talked about her concern that when she typed children's dictated sentences on the computer, the children did not seem to understand that it was their own words that appeared on the screen— even if they seemed to make this print-speech connection when she recorded their dictation with pencil and paper. Barbara described the problem for the teachers and researchers to consider together.

> There's something about that screen. The connection doesn't seem to be there. When you draw their attention to the screen [and say] "This is the word. Watch the word," and "This is what you're telling me" or . . . if the word is repeated, I'll say, "This is that word," you know, "You can type this in now." I just don't always feel that they're getting that connection.

A researcher asked if the teacher said each word aloud as she typed it, and Barbara responded that she did. As the researcher working with Barbara, I added that while some children were looking at the screen in what looked like anticipation that something would appear, others were watching Barbara's fingers, or the wall, or something else, and resisted all of her attempts to call their attention to the words appearing on the screen. Debby added:

> They don't really believe that hitting that key is what's making that letter come up on there. They probably think that in that screen is something magical. . . . I think a lot of them know that when you're writing on the chart or they're writing on their papers that they're—they or you— are making those words. I can see where [words on a screen] would be abstract to them.

In exchanges like this one, the researchers believed that the teachers and researchers constructed tentative understandings of phenomena that were new to all of them and together generated knowledge of using word processing with beginning writers.

The teachers, however, initially viewed these meetings as generating knowledge for the researchers only. Their colleagues' experiences were considered to have little bearing on their own work. Comments such as "These concerns are more for their levels" or "I don't have that problem" were common in the first five monthly meetings. When, in response to what was beginning to seem to the researchers like an extraordinary amount of after-school meeting time, the director of the research project suggested that we request that the school district grant regular released time for our meetings, the teachers argued that meeting during released time was neither possible nor necessary. After several plans for meeting without doing so on personal time were proposed and rejected, Bev broke in and asked, "Are you all having problems getting information?" When the researchers protested that this was hardly the case and that in fact, they were "drowning in data," she continued, "I was just thinking—is this what you want? More information from us? Do you need to know more from me?" After further assurances that this was not the case, she added, "Well, now that that's clear . . ." and suggested we continue with the discussion. We did, and it was decided that we should continue to hold the monthly meetings after school.

Throughout most of the first year, the teachers and researchers differed in their perceptions of the purposes and value of the meetings. Not until the second year of the research project were meetings viewed as serving the interests of the teachers as well as researchers. Although it is not possible to determine from the data whether this shift in perception was due to the mix of experienced and new teachers or to the teachers' and researchers' growing understanding of each other's purposes, it is clear that the meetings came to be viewed, at least by some, in a new light. Barbara and Debby, the two teachers new to the project, routinely used the monthly research meetings as opportunities to check their experiences against those of their more experienced colleagues. When she joined the project, Debby asked about the possibility of meeting regularly; at the end of the project, Barbara asked if we could continue to meet over the summmer.

Summer word-processing workshops. Prior to the initiation of the research project, the researchers planned a summer workshop to introduce the teachers to the hardware and software, to explore teaching writing with word processing, to discuss goals for the children and what role word processing might play in meeting them, and to provide further information about the research project. The workshop was scheduled for five full days on the university campus. The teachers were paid stipends to attend.

The workshop was conducted by the three researchers—a professor of language arts and the director of the teacher education program that placed practicum students in the teachers' classrooms, a field supervisor of those students, and an instructor in the computer education program at the university. The teachers were already familiar with the first two researchers; they did not meet the third until the summer workshop. The workshop activities for the first day, modeled after those used in the researchers' college classes, included structured word processing tasks and writing workshop activities. The researchers took on the role of experts, instructing the teachers in skills that the researchers had determined the teachers would need.

The teachers met this agenda with resistance. In several hours of discussion at the beginning of the second day, they voiced their dissatisfaction. They questioned the appropriateness of spending workshop time on their own writing, and questioned the feasibility of ever using word processing in their classrooms. Consequently, later the same day the researchers altered the course of the workshop to include more informal discussion of goals and anticipated problems, more time for teacher-researcher pairs to work together on individual teachers' interests and needs, and less full-group instruction. Much of the time was devoted to exploring the logistic problems the teachers raised and jointly constructing possible solutions. Although the problems raised were serious and demanded immediate attention, they also represented larger ideological conflicts stemming from differences in how the researchers and teachers viewed curriculum knowledge and teachers' roles (see Chapter 5 for a fuller discussion).

In the second year, the researchers used what they had learned in the first workshop to design different introductory experiences for the two teachers joining the project. Barbara and Debby explored the hardware and software in their homes over the summer, calling on their colleagues or the researchers for assistance as needed. Then they attended a week-long workshop that addressed their questions about the equipment and the research project. Barbara and Debby spent two days with the researchers, sharing information about the research project and about the routines and curriculum in their classrooms. For the remaining three days, the three teachers who had participated in the project in the previous year joined the workshop to share their experiences and answer questions posed by their colleagues.

The initial plans for the way in which the first summer workshop would be conducted resembled typical school district inservice workshops in which curriculum knowledge was delivered to teachers. The way the first workshop actually unfolded, and the plans for the second workshop, more closely resembled the established procedures of dialogue and sharing that characterized the ways in which the teachers gained and passed on curriculum knowledge in the school.

Ideology

The researchers' beliefs were revealed in formal statements of assumptions in published papers, in individual journals and field notes, in collective decisions made in meetings about research design and procedures, and in individual interactions with the teachers and the principal. In some cases, the ideology of the researchers was compatible with those of the school and the school district. In some cases, it differed. And in some cases, the researchers' practices were inconsistent with their own espoused beliefs.

Curriculum. The researchers assumed that curriculum is not a fixed, generalizable product created in advance of teaching, but a personal and situated process negotiated in response to children's and teachers' strengths, needs, goals and perceptions, and the demands, supports, and constraints of the context. Consequently, no content or achievement requirements or timetables were given to guide or constrain the teachers' curriculum work. Nor was the summer workshop used to develop a common curriculum to be taught by all. Instead, it was seen as an opportunity for the teachers to explore what the technology had to offer, to learn to manage the system, and to consider its potential to meet their curriculum goals. The researchers assumed the most appropriate and effective curriculum would be created in the context of the teachers' classroom practice.

Curriculum knowledge. The researchers believed that important curriculum knowledge was generated by teachers in the daily work of teaching and learning with their children. The absence in the literature of expert knowledge on how to teach and apply word processing in the elementary grades was not seen as an impediment to the project's efforts. In fact, it was assumed that the teachers had the accumulated expertise necessary to create appropriate and effective word-processing curricula and to devise ways to incorporate word processing into other parts of their teaching. However, when considering how the teachers would learn to use the hardware and software—a far less complex task than creating word-processing curriculum—the researchers cast teachers in the roles of passive receivers of direct instruction in knowledge that the researchers determined the teachers did not have and would need.

Teachers' roles. Finally, the researchers expressed a belief in an active role for teachers in both research and in curriculum making. They conceived of the teacher's role in research as a source as well as a critic of data, and created mechanisms for sharing and thinking about data together regularly. In curriculum matters, they conceived of teachers as creators and critics of curriculum knowledge and therefore provided flexible, malleable curriculum tools rather than prescriptive curriculum materials.

In their views of curriculum, curriculum knowledge, and teachers' roles in relation to both, the researchers' ideology was more consistent with that of the school than that of the school district. Like the principal, the researchers provided teachers with material and collegial support to create their curricula rather than prescribing a curriculum for them. And unlike the school district context, interactions in the research project context were characterized by ongoing negotiations rather than fixed policies. Researchers' assumptions were tested and challenged, and consequently some research policies and practices underwent striking transformations.

SUMMARY

The contexts of the teachers' curriculum work were complex and inter-related. They reached outward from the classroom to the contexts of the research project, the school, and the school district; back into the histories of groups and organizations; and down into the underlying ideologies that guided and were revealed in each.

Policies and practices, as well as dominant ideologies, in one context were often inconsistent with those in another context. Figure 3.2 summarizes the characteristics of each context found to be significant to the teachers in their work as active agents in curriculum creation and critique. The top half of the figure includes policies and practices that had an impact on their work. In some cases, practices in one context directly interfered with or contradicted those in another. For example, curriculum standardization policies in the school district and practices that supported individual curriculum initiatives in the school context were in direct conflict. So too were the summer word-processing workshop and the established practice in the school of teachers' active participation in generating and sharing curriculum knowledge. The bottom half of the figure summarizes the dominant assumptions about curriculum, curriculum knowledge, and teachers' relation to both. It is here that conflicts and contradictions are most marked.

Figure 3.2 *Policies and practices and dominant ideologies in the three contexts: School district, school, and research project*

	School District	School	Research Project
Policies/Practices	• Curriculum standardization • District wide in-service training procedures	• Individual curriculum initiatives • "In-servicing ourselves" and the "natural" spread of curriculum knowledge	• Selection of curriculum materials • Weekly observations • Monthly research meetings • Summer word-processing workshops
Dominant Ideologies	• Curriculum as context-independent product • Curriculum knowledge as created and delivered to teachers through direct instruction by experts • Teachers' role as "rational adopter" of curriculum created and delivered by experts	• Curriculum as a process negotiated in the classroom context, guided by but not determined by the "outline of outcomes" provided by the school district • Curriculum knowledge as created by teachers in the context of their daily work in classrooms and/or passed on by a colleague • Teachers' role as initiator of curriculum change and creator of curriculum knowledge	• Curriculum as personal and context-dependent process • Curriculum knowledge as created by teachers in the context of their daily work in classrooms • Teachers' role as creator and critic of curriculum knowledge

It was within these multiple and conflicting contexts that the teachers actively engaged in the work of creating and critiquing curriculum. Yet it was through the lenses of their own beliefs and assumptions that the teachers perceived and negotiated their work within their own classrooms. In the next chapter we return to the teachers and take a closer look at the ideologies underlying their work.

4 Teachers' Ideologies and Classroom Curriculum Work

In Chapter 2, each teacher was introduced against the backdrop of her ongoing curriculum work. The portraits were designed to capture norms of the teachers' classroom practice, and the assumptions, goals, and values that guided and gave meaning to each teacher's practice. In the preceding chapter, the teachers' collective assumptions about curriculum policies and practices in the contexts of the school district, school, and research project were examined. In this chapter, we address the teachers' shared beliefs and assumptions, which not only guided their day-to-day curriculum decisions, but also formed the lenses through which they perceived and reacted to the policies and practices in the school district, school, and research project as they influenced their classroom curriculum work.

The teachers' explicit assumptions were identified in their direct statements of beliefs in meetings, journals, interviews, and informal conversations. Tacit beliefs, not so readily accessible, were brought to the fore when routine practices were challenged. Apple (1979) asserts that "basic assumptions . . . normally known only tacitly, remain unspoken and are very difficult to formulate explicitly . . . and only become problematic when a previously routine situation becomes significantly altered" (p. 126). The teachers' routine practices were being disrupted in at least three ways at the time of the study: they received at least one new standardized curriculum each year, they were engaged in introducing word processing into their teaching, and they were participants in a university-based research project. The teachers' tacit assumptions were uncovered and made available for examination as they assessed required curricula, devised their own word-processing curricula, and discussed their decisions about both in regular meetings with researchers and colleagues.

A complex array of assumptions shape teachers' curriculum work (Colletti, 1987; Connelly & Clandinin, 1988; Stodolsky, 1989; Yonemura, 1986). Among them are assumptions about children and how they learn and what constitutes good teaching. These and other assumptions influenced the teachers' deliberations over the word-processing curricula they created and the standardized curricula they received. For example, Debby believed that children learn effectively when teaching and being taught by other children. Consequently, she arranged many opportunities for her children to coach classmates, teach other third graders, and assist younger children in writing and using word processing. Margaret believed that repeated exposure to new skills was fundamental to learning, so she brought pairs of children to the word processor to learn editing skills. While one worked, the other watched so that each had an opportunity to "see it twice."

Yet other assumptions having to do with wider issues of curriculum and role pervaded the teachers' discussion of and writing about their curriculum work as well. These assumptions concerned the nature of curriculum, the nature and genesis of curriculum knowledge, and the process of changing curriculum. Whereas each teacher held her own individual assumptions about children, learning, and teaching, assumptions about curriculum and role were strikingly consistent across the data on each teacher. Furthermore, these assumptions applied both to the curriculum they created in their own classrooms and to the mandated standardized curriculum. In order to understand the teachers' curriculum work in context, it is necessary to attend to these assumptions.

THE NATURE OF CURRICULUM

The teachers' discussions of their curriculum work revealed two related but distinct categories of curriculum—"the curriculum" and "my curriculum." The distinction was a critical one. "The curriculum" was used to refer to the collection of school district documents that prescribed content, goals, materials, and, in some cases, activities and amount of instructional time in each subject area. "The curriculum," as used by the teachers, was similar to the terms "formal curriculum" (Goodlad, Klein, & Tye, 1979) and "written curriculum" (Glatthorn, 1987), in that it referred to curriculum that was created outside the classroom prior to the point of instruction by someone other than the classroom teacher. However, the similarity was limited to these surface features only. Whereas in prevailing conceptions of curriculum, teachers and children are cast as objects of others' curriculum making, the teachers conceived of their role in relation to curriculum produced and mandated by others as one of active agency in which they and their students were subjects in, rather than objects of, curriculum and curriculum making.

The teachers' conception of "my curriculum" was more inclusive, more cohesive, and less static than "the curriculum." It encompassed all of the day-to-day classroom experiences jointly constructed by the teachers and their children and was related, in fundamental ways, to conceptions of curriculum as enacted (Snyder, Bolin, & Zumwalt, 1992) and experiential curriculum

(Goodlad et al., 1979). "My curriculum" referred to decisions made before and during an activity about what to teach, and also how, when, to whom, and with what materials to teach. It included decisions about what content to emphasize, what values to stress, what social and emotional qualities to nurture, which children to support, which children to challenge, and how to organize space, time, and children into groups. It was not considered to be separate and distinct from "the curriculum," but a superordinate category of curriculum that took in and subsumed "the curriculum."

The terms that will be used here to mark the distinction between "the" and "my" curriculum were chosen to reflect the active agency the teachers assumed for themselves in their conceptions of curriculum. I will refer to "the curriculum" as "received curriculum" to emphasize that the teachers conceived of it as curriculum to be taken in and acted upon. I will use the term "enacted curriculum," as Snyder, Bolin, and Zumwalt (1992) use, to represent the day-to-day classroom experiences jointly constructed and enacted by teachers and their children.

The teachers' assumptions about the nature of curriculum were not limited to descriptive assumptions that distinguished between enacted and received curricula. They also held normative assumptions that delineated what they believed curriculum should be. Two such assumptions proved critical in their work with both enacted and received curricula: that curriculum was to be a coherent whole and that curriculum was malleable. All curriculum, enacted or received, was measured against these assumptions and, wherever possible, was made to conform to the teachers' normative beliefs.

Curriculum as a Coherent Whole

The teachers assumed curriculum to be made up of interdependent parts that were logically connected and philosophically consistent. Content taught in one subject area was applied or related to other subjects, and content and method in all subject areas were based on related pedagogical beliefs and directed toward related goals. This conception of curriculum differed significantly from that on which the school district's curriculum standardization policies appeared to be based. Those policies assumed a curriculum comprised of discrete, self-contained subject-area modules that could be evaluated, removed, and replaced independently and without consideration of the existing classroom curricula into which it was introduced or from which it was removed.

The teachers, however, did not treat subject-area curricula as discrete wholes, but created connnections among them. Margaret's unit of study on colonial life, for example, linked social studies, language arts, and science content. Similarly, Margaret's and Barbara's practices of aligning science and social studies lessons with related stories in the basal reading text were demonstrations of the interdependence of content in their classroom curricula.

Although theirs were not fully integrated curricula in which distinctions between subject areas did not exist, theirs were coherent curricula in which logical linkages between subject areas were consciously made.

Furthermore, the teachers assumed that the content and method in each curriculum area should reflect a coherent set of beliefs about children, teaching, and learning and should be directed toward compatible goals. Barbara's concerns about the newly mandated writing curriculum came from her belief that all parts of her curriculum should support the development of her children's positive sense of themselves as learners. The writing curriculum was seen as interfering with the accomplishment of this goal, or as she said, "defeating [her] very purposes."

In the process of constructing her own word-processing curriculum, Barbara also struggled to do so in ways that furthered rather than hampered her children's progress toward her established goals. The computer keyboard, labeled in capital letters, raised for Barbara what she called a "very perplexing problem" of conflicting goals. Word processing supported her commitment to valuing her children's statements and stories by giving her a tool to easily produce captions for their drawings, recollections from their field trips, and bound books of their stories. It enabled her children to see the connection between their spoken words and words in print as their dictated stories appeared on the screen. And it allowed her children who were struggling to print legible letters that were positioned correctly on lines to feel the success of producing a perfect-looking text. Yet she was concerned that seeing only capital letters on the keyboard might reinforce her children's dependence on these known letter forms and slow their learning to recognize and use lowercase letters. For two days she pondered this problem. She brought the problem to the research group and several acceptable solutions were offered, all of which included in some way adding lowercase letters to the keyboard. In her thanks to the group she explained that this was such a "big problem" for her because as long as the keyboard "wasn't fitting into what I was trying to do, theoretically, everything fell apart."

The assumption of a coherent curriculum led teachers to carefully assess all alterations or additions to their established curricula. Each new part had to be consistent with the content, beliefs, and goals on which their ongoing practice was based. When received curricula or curricula the teachers introduced themselves were inconsistent with their ongoing practice, it was assumed that the curricula could be changed.

Curriculum as Malleable

The teachers brought to their curriculum work the assumption that curriculum was neither static nor unassailable, but malleable. Furthermore, it was assumed that it was within their role as teachers to shape, reshape, and adapt it to their own and their children's evolving needs and interests. Received curriculum and enacted curriculum were continuously evaluated and modified in response to the ever-changing contexts in which they conducted their work. In the case of received curriculum, the teachers routinely critiqued its content, goals, and methods. Theirs were not idle complaints, but well-reasoned assessments that led to modifications. Although the teachers varied somewhat in the ways and the degree to which they altered the curriculum that was required of them, they each took an active stance, acting on the curriculum rather than allowing it to determine their activity.

The teachers' beliefs about the malleability of received curriculum were viable because the curriculum and instruction organization in the school district, as in any school district, could not, in fact, enforce its curriculum mandates for standardized practice. As a "loosely coupled system" (Weick, 1976), the curriculum and instruction organization functioned at a great enough distance to permit the teachers to continuously alter received curriculum. However, the extent to which the teachers made modifications was bounded by their perceptions of what the system would bear. For example, the teachers worked around district priorities by placing emphasis where they felt it appropriate and giving cursory treatment to required curricula that they did not value or deemed otherwise inappropriate. They also overlapped mandated minutes of instruction—incorporating writing into a science lesson, for example—to gain time to allocate to content that they believed was of equal or greater value to their particular children.

> You have to teach within [the mandated curriculum]. You can adapt and teach your own way and integrate it or whatever, but you have to do that on your own. Like they say, 18 hours of this and 12 of that—you can't do that. You have to put things together, but you don't tell them that you're doing that.

And required assignments were completed hastily.

> Now that all the . . . required assignments are out of the way we can do what we want!

They also ignored what they felt they could. Referring to the prewriting activities included in the district's writing curriculum guide, a teacher assessed them and decided to "just use my own ideas." Looking at the entire grade-level curriculum another decided,

> I made my own rules. . . . It [mandated curriculum] was not appropriate. . . . We covered the required skills in our own way.

Although the teachers adapted and ignored mandated curriculum, there were points at which they did not challenge the system. For example, a teacher who did not believe that children's writing should be graded expressed her disagreement with this policy:

> We have to give a letter grade for how the kids write. And that, that's always toughest for me. I do my entire report card and I do [those grades] last. And I would love to leave them blank but I'm not allowed. Almost all my kids do well in writing because they all write! So how could they get a C or D in writing?

She complied with the grading requirement, however, by assigning relatively high marks to most of her children. She knew the requirement was firm and the consequences for noncompliance too great for her to do otherwise. Similarly, all of the teachers completed and submitted the writing assignments that were required by the school district each year, although they often did so with expressions of relief. When they judged that the consequences of ignoring or altering the mandated curriculum were too great, they chose compliance—even minimal compliance—over defiance.

In order to adapt curricula to respond to a continuously changing context and to maintain the philosophic coherence of their curriculum, the teachers needed to be aware of the boundaries within which they could make their modifications. Consequently, teachers tended to follow a newly mandated curriculum carefully at first in order to learn its demands, as well as to extend their own curriculum knowledge. Debby described her first year teaching third grade as a time of getting to know that grade level's reading curriculum and of not straying far from what was required. Bev, it will be recalled, uncharacteristically sought exact prescriptions to follow when she was first required to teach writing. She looked for rules to guide her work and questioned neither the content nor the method of the prescribed writing program. But once Bev had clear information about what outcomes were expected of her and a backlog of experience teaching and observing her children, she too applied her own knowledge, goals, and values to critiquing and modifying the required curriculum.

The teachers defined curriculum as a dynamic process rather than a reified product. They conceived of curriculum as a unified whole woven together with logical linkages of content in the subject areas and by their own pedagogical beliefs and goals. They also regarded curriculum as a revisable entity to be continually shaped and reshaped by them to be consistent with their own ideologies and changing contexts. Assumed within their definition of curriculum was the role of teacher as active agent. Teacher agency was also prominent in their assumptions about the nature and sources of curriculum knowledge.

THE NATURE AND GENESIS OF CURRICULUM KNOWLEDGE

Work by Shulman (1987) and others suggests that knowledge of curriculum constitutes an identifiable part of teachers' professional knowledge. Of the four types of professional knowledge that Shulman identifies, three are relevant to this discussion of teachers' work with word processing in their curricula: content knowledge, in this case knowledge of writing and using word processing; pedagogical content knowledge, or knowledge of how to shape representations and experiences that convey how one creates a piece of writing and masters the skill of word processing; and curricular knowledge, or knowledge of the capabilities of word processing as they apply to teaching writing. Together these constitute what is referred to here as "curriculum knowledge."

Curriculum knowledge differs in its genesis and character from what Schwab (1969) refers to as the "theoretical knowledge" traditionally held by academics in the curriculum field. Theoretical knowledge, he argues, is concerned primarily with reaching "warranted conclusions" and is an insufficient base on which to build a viable curriculum. "Practical knowledge," he asserts, is required to supplement theoretical curriculum knowledge. Work by Connelly and Clandinin (1985, 1988), Elbaz (1983), Yonemura et al., (1986), and Shulman (1987) documents the breadth and intricacies of the teacher's knowledge of curriculum that Schwab would identify as practical knowledge. It is to this conception of curriculum knowledge as practical knowledge that the teachers in this study subscribed.

Curriculum Knowledge as Practical, Situated, and Personal

Schwab (1969) describes practical knowledge as that which is acquired through "deliberation," "defensible decisions," and "purposed action" (p. 2). He emphasizes that "practical knowledge" is in no way to be construed as less analytic than "theoretical knowledge." It is distinguished instead by the fact that it is intimately tied to the context in which it is generated and applied. It is, according to Schwab,

> brought to bear not in some archetypical classroom but in a particular locus in time and space with smells, shadows, seats, and conditions outside its walls which may have much to do with what is achieved inside. Above all, the supposed beneficiary is not the generic child, not even a class or kind of child out of the psychological or sociological literature pertaining to the child. The beneficiaries will consist of very local kinds of children and, within the local kinds, individual children. (p. 12)

Whereas theoretical curriculum knowledge arises from the assumptions of particular disciplines, practical curriculum knowledge is grounded in particular settings.

More recently, Scribner's (1984) study of dairy workers, Schon's (1983) work on reflective practice in the professions, and Sternberg and Caruso's (1985) delineation of practical modes of knowing describe the situation-specific nature of practical knowledge. Smith and Geoffrey (1968) assert that much of teachers' work could be characterized as "situational thinking." Elbaz (1983) determined that teacher's knowledge of curriculum is oriented to a particular context, and Connelly and Clandinin (1985, 1988) characterize teachers' curriculum knowledge as "embodied in the history, the moment and the act" (p. 178). Because it is so intimately tied to particular events and points in time, situated knowledge is not static, or reified, but is always in process (Elbaz, 1983; Brown, Collins, & Duguid, 1989). Just as over time contexts shift, problems evolve, and students grow, curriculum knowledge is always changing.

The teachers shared this view of curriculum knowledge as practical, situated knowledge that is continually in revision in response to shifting conditions. The evolution of Margaret's thinking about what word processing skills to teach, how to teach them, and to whom is representative of her colleagues' conceptions of curriculum knowledge as situated and practical. In an interview in the middle of her second year of work with word processing, Margaret considered her current work with word processing in light of the content and methods of instruction she had developed in the previous year. In this second year of work with word processing, Margaret's content knowledge, or mastery of word processing procedures, had grown significantly. Her pedagogical content knowledge, or knowledge of how to create situations in which children could acquire knowledge of the capabilities and procedures of word processing, was expanding, as was her curricular knowledge, or knowlege of how to apply word-processing capabilities to the task of teaching writing. But her class in the second year was, as a group, less mature and less capable than the group of children she had taught in the previous year, and she was dealing with the new basal reading series for the first time as well. Margaret said,

> I'm not doing as much this year. Because of the new reading series and because of the type of class I have this year—it's kind of difficult. . . .
>   Some I have to watch more carefully because they could be destructive, and those children don't use [the computer] much. And the others, who are better behaved and more capable on it, use it more.
>   I don't worry as much about how many turns each child gets. I'm no longer trying to keep track and making sure that everybody gets an equal turn. I just don't think that it's important. . . . Whoever happens to be ready to write, writes. So you don't have to worry about waiting for somebody, or see who has had a turn or who hasn't had a turn or see who hasn't finished a workbook. . . .

> I have not *taught* them as much this year. I started out the year teaching the specific lessons to the reading groups. I taught lessons on using the spacebar, using the shift key . . . I did save and print [procedures]. . . .
>
> Then after the first two months I even stopped doing that. Whatever they have learned, they have picked up from each other, or from working on it themselves, or from working with Jessica [the researcher]. . . . As a matter of fact, I think that some of these children can find the letter keys and type faster than the children last year. . . . Last year they would complain that it was easier to write in their journals because it was faster. These children would prefer to use the computer.

With greater demands on her time and attention, knowledge of what and how to teach that was regarded as valid in the previous year was rejected or revised in the second year. Whereas in the first year equal access to the computer and direct instruction for each child in a common body of word processing skills was found to be appropriate and effective, a more relaxed approach to computer access, and initial instruction in only the most basic skills of entering text, were appropriate and proved to be at least as effective. The curriculum knowledge that was regarded as valid was that which was proven to be appropriate and effective in a particular context at a particular point in time.

Curriculum knowledge has also been described as personal knowledge (Connelly & Clandinin, 1988). Personal knowledge of curriculum is subjective knowledge embedded in teachers' personal histories as teachers and learners and is built on their individual perspectives, conceptions, constructs, and theories. Bev's early encounters with teaching kindergarten children to write are illustrative. She had always modeled writing for her children by recording their "morning news" on the chalk board in perfect letters and standard spellings. Bulletin board and wall displays and labels on furniture, supplies, and equipment provided correct spellings of color words, number words, children's names, and the names of objects in the room. Although she had never taught a formal writing curriculum, Bev had accumulated personal knowledge of ways to systematically expose kindergarten children to print and of how children responded to those experiences. The school district's insistence that she encourage children to use invented spellings clashed with her personal knowledge of early literacy activities with children. It also raised memories of debates early in her career over the advisability of using the Initial Teaching Alphabet (ITA) with a separate symbol for each speech sound. She questioned whether the children would have to "unlearn" their invented phonetic spellings in much the same way as it was believed children would have to unlearn the nonstandard ITA symbols before they could learn standard spellings. The new knowledge Bev subsequently constructed about young children and writing, like the knowledge she brought to this task, was shaped by her personal professional history and theories about children and print.

In their work with both enacted and received curriculum, the teachers regarded curriculum knowledge as practical rather than theoretical, situated rather than generalizable across contexts, and highly personalized. Their assumptions did not merely describe what they believed to be true about curriculum knowledge, but served as standards against which they measured the relative worth of curriculum knowledge. Curriculum knowledge generated in the teachers' own contexts and confirmed by their own experiences was valued over knowledge created by others in other contexts. The nature of curriculum knowledge the teachers assumed implied that teachers would take a central role in creating it.

The Genesis of Curriculum Knowledge

Curriculum knowledge was assumed to be created by teachers in interaction with students and content in particular contexts. It was assumed that valid curriculum knowledge was generated when teachers created their own curricula and acted on received curriculum. In both cases, it was the teacher who was the creator and critic of curriculum knowledge.

Creating and enacting curriculum. Debby's journal provides glimpses of the ways in which the teachers acted on the assumption that valid curriculum knowledge was created in teachers' classroom interactions. In this excerpt, she deals with the questions of which word-processing skills were necessary and appropriate to teach her third-grade students and how best to provide instruction in those skills. Based on colleagues' and researchers' observations that keyboarding presented difficulties to some children, she planned to begin with basic typing instruction. Debby planned several short lessons in which children would learn the home keys and practice using proper fingering by using cardboard replicas of the computer keyboard. Following the first lesson, she wrote:

> I noticed immediately that they were most comfortable using only one finger. . . . I told them that that was O.K. but they should really try to use two fingers—one on the right and one on the left. . . .
> So I reflected [on this] later in the day and decided that I do not want them to become expert typists, but I do think it will be beneficial to them to know [the location of] the keys.

Just as she created and re-created knowledge of what content was appropriate to teach, she generated her own knowledge of appropriate teaching methods.

After a subsequent lesson in which children practiced typing words listed on the chalk board, she noted:

> Most of them followed right along with me. Some were faster and some slower. The biggest problem I found was that some of the kids were bored! I asked them to bear with the rest of us.

She limited later practice periods to 10 minutes and children who completed the list of practice words early were sent back to their desks to begin another activity.

Colleagues with more experience than Debby in using word processing with children had grappled with questions of what keyboarding skills were necessary and appropriate to teach elementary school children and had devised procedures to teach those skills. Their work had clearly informed Debby's planning. Her colleagues had alerted her to the difficulties keyboarding posed for some children. One colleague had created the cardboard keyboards and devised effective means of using them to develop a wide range of word processing skills. Although Debby did not adopt the content or methods of her colleagues, their experiences were the foundation on which she proceeded to create her own knowledge about teaching word processing to her children.

There are those who would argue that teachers' re-creation of knowledge that others already hold represents a duplication of effort, resulting in waste and inefficiency. Kerr (1987), however, argues that highly complex, context-dependent tasks, like teaching, characterized by "non-recurrent circumstances," are not amenable to the seemingly more efficient practice of providing ready-made knowledge. She cites Elmore and asserts that, when considering teachers' curriculum work, "redundancy is in fact crucial" (p. 30) to the efficient and expert performance of teaching. Expert teachers create and re-create knowledge of how to make particular behavior, attitudes, and content accessible and meaningful to individual students at particular points in time. But they do not do so in a vacuum.

Acting on received curriculum knowledge. Not all curriculum knowledge must or can be generated by the individual teacher within her own classroom. Curriculum knowledge that is generated by others—subject matter specialists, curriculum developers, and colleagues, for example—contributes to the content knowledge and general pedagogical knowledge identified by Shulman (1987) as among the critical components of teachers' knowledge base. For example, curriculum guidelines such as those provided by the National Council of Teachers of Mathematics, the National Council of Teachers of English, the American Association for the Advancement of Science, or the work of learning theorists, represent such knowledge. But this knowledge, too, must be brought to bear on the particular context in which each teacher conducts her work. While creating and acting on curriculum knowledge, teachers interpret it, shape it, and adapt it to their particular contexts (Ben-Peretz, 1990). It then becomes part of the teachers' situated, personal, practical, curriculum knowledge.

Bev's responses to the instruction she received in how to teach her kindergarten children to write illustrates well the ways in which the teachers regarded others' knowledge of what and how to teach. After an initial period of doubt and dependence on explicit instructions for how to proceed, Bev began to question the appropriateness of the goals, content, and methods of teaching writing presented in the workshops. She tested the procedures she was given and based her assessments on her children's products and performances. She took what she was taught in the school district workshops, drew on her experiences with the informal writing activities she had done in the past such as the dictation of daily "news," incorporated what she knew about children in general and about her current class of children in particular, attended to how each successive writing activity unfolded and how each child's writing skills progressed, and created her own knowledge of how to teach kindergarten children to write.

In the case of word processing, however, the teachers had few outside sources from which to seek knowledge of how or even what to teach beginning writers about word processing. Nothing was available to them in the form of national guidelines or school district curriculum guides, and the professional literature provided little guidance (Cochran-Smith, 1991). The experiences of their colleagues provided their only external sources of curriculum knowledge. Yet this, too, was regarded as knowledge to be interpreted and adapted to their own situation. When Debby noted, "I got a lot of good ideas. I took some of Margaret's, some of Bev's . . . and came up with my own way," a researcher replied that it appeared that she then abandoned at least half of those ideas. She explained that they "weren't working" for her so she adapted them and did what she felt was best for her and for her children.

The teachers in this study shared the assumption that curriculum knowledge is practical knowledge, that it is context-dependent and includes both knowledge that is created by teachers and knowledge that is acquired and interpreted by teachers. Collectively, the teachers perceived their roles in relation to the curriculum and the genesis of curriculum knowledge in active terms, as initiating, generating, critiquing, and adapting curriculum. An awareness of the teachers' assumptions about their active relationship to curriculum prepares one to understand more fully their assumptions about the processes of curriculum change.

THE NATURE OF CURRICULUM CHANGE

Implicit in each teacher's assumptions about curriculum and curriculum knowledge was the concept of continuous change. Whereas curriculum change is regarded in the literature as something done *to* curriculum, the teachers defined the ongoing creation and introduction of new curriculum, and the adaptation of existing curriculum, into their conception of curriculum itself. Rather than viewing curriculum change as an action, event, or process interjected into or overlayed onto the day-to-day curriculum work of teachers, the teachers conceived of change as an integral part of their ongoing curriculum work.

Change was necessary, in the teachers' judgement, to accommodate the needs of their children as learners and themselves as teachers. It was required to make curriculum responsive to the very particular and ever-changing needs of their children, and necessary, as well, for their own satisfaction and professional growth as teachers.

Altering Curriculum in Response to Children's Needs

The teachers' beliefs in the malleability of curriculum and in its situated nature, and their assumptions of a philosophically coherent curriculum and the necessity of shaping curriculum to be consistent with their pedagogical beliefs and goals, were all brought to the task of making curriculum responsive to children's needs. The following excerpts from Barbara's discussion of her language arts program illustrate the way in which the influence of such beliefs was evident in one teacher's consideration of the standardized language arts materials.

> The way I approached [teaching language arts] was not the same as [the district administrators] would have approached it. I made my own rules. I didn't use the book the other language arts groups used. It was not appropriate, but I think we covered [the skills] in our own way. We talked about capital letters and we still talked about periods and all the things that you're supposed to cover in first grade. . . .
>
> I don't think anybody ever really felt down about themselves or what they were doing. Adhering rigidly to district guidelines with regard to curriculum blows my mind, because I don't see the success. It seems totally irrational to me to set up something that we know kids are going to bomb on.

Her knowledge of her children and her belief in the importance of success for every child made alteration of the received curriculum a professional necessity.

Barbara and her colleagues also believed that curriculum was to be continually altered and refined to fit the needs of new classes each year and to match the growth of a particular class over the course of a year. Changing curriculum over years or months, as well as adapting lessons in progress on the basis of on-the-spot observations of their children, were all assumed in the teachers' conceptions of curriculum and of their roles as teachers.

Altering Curriculum in Response to Teachers' Needs

Not only did the teachers believe in the necessity of changing and creating curricula to meet the needs of their children, they also believed in the necessity of altering what and how they taught to satisfy their own needs. Margaret explained:

> I like to change because I can't stand to do the same thing year after year. And I'll change some of [the first year's work with word processing] next year. I'll do things a lot differently than I did this year.

Bev described how she had enthusiastically developed one year's curriculum around a series of projects, only to develop new ones the following year. She apologetically attributed this to her inability to keep organized records that would allow her to reproduce her teaching from year to year.

> I'm not that organized a person—that I do thus and thus every year. . . . I do things differently every single year. I've had years that I say I'm into art. I mean one year I used to have art activities and they would rotate and do a different one each day at the tables. That worked out. And I thought that was terrific, but I didn't do it the next year. I did something else.

But she speaks of those times when she "never did the same thing two years in a row" as exciting times in her teaching.

Debby looked forward to altering curriculum as a source of challenge as well as excitement. Once she was familiar with the required curriculum and materials for the third grade, she felt ready for a new challenge and regarded the prospect of learning to use word processing as "exciting and fun." She saw learning a new teaching skill and as a way to channel the "excess energy" she felt she had after the hectic previous year. She explained, "It's just one more new thing, so I'm really excited."

In addition, initiating curriculum changes that involved learning something new was valued as a means of stretching one's capabilities and stimulating professional growth. Barbara wrote in her journal: "I think I have continued to grow professionally in terms of designing and redesigning my educational program." The teachers actively sought the opportunities for variety, stimulation, challenge, and increasing their abilities to meet their children's needs that changing their curricula provided. Introducing word processing into their curricula was perceived by the teachers as such an opportunity. Yet the teachers objected to references to their work with word processing as "curriculum change."

Change and Continuity with Current Practice

When I framed questions that suggested that introducing word processing into their teaching could be labeled as a significant "change" in their practice, the teachers responded with surprise or denial. They claimed simply that their work with word processing did not represent "change." Their reactions were puzzling. What I identified as change—teaching the new skills required to use the word processors, devising new assignments that took advantage of the unique characteristics of the computer, and adapting schedules and procedures to accommodate the fact that not all children could use the computers at the same time—was denied, minimized, overlooked, or explained away by the teachers. The teachers did not experience these alterations as instances of curriculum change. Each protested that she was "not doing anything that I wasn't doing all along." Yet from the perspective of an outside observer, their curricula had changed significantly.

Bussis, Chittenden, and Amarel (1976) make a distinction between surface curriculum and teachers' assumptions underlying curriculum that is useful here. They define the "surface structure" of the curriculum as what an observer would note in a lesson or a class day. Below the surface curriculum, however, is a "deep structure" defined as the "organizing content" that encompasses the teacher's values and goals. For the teachers, the concept of "curriculum change" included more than surface changes in practice. The assumptions underlying altered practices were more important than the surface features of those practices. If alterations in the surface content of their practice were consistent with their values and goals, as well as with their beliefs about teaching and learning, the alterations were experienced as continuous with their ongoing practice of curriculum revision and adaptation and therefore were not experienced as "change." On the other hand, if alterations were inconsistent with teachers' organizing content or ideologies, or if they blocked opportunities for teachers to act on their own values, beliefs, or goals, they were viewed negatively and identified as instances of "curriculum change."

Incorporation of word processing into the teachers' curricula was experienced as continuous with their ongoing curriculum work. Their methods of teaching word processing and the uses they made of it were consistent with the goals and values underlying their current practice. For example, Barbara made it clear that she decided to use word processing to enhance her established language experience approach to teaching literary skills. Later in her first year of using word processing, we discussed some of the changes she was experiencing in her teaching—the changing population in the school and the standardized curriculum. When I added word processing to the list of changes, Barbara interrupted to explain that *this* was not a change:

> . . . the way we use [word processing] fits into the whole program. I mean, I don't see that as being different. I don't do things with it that don't really seem appropriate to me and for my program. . . . As far as I'm concerned, the word processor, that's not new. I mean we didn't have the computers to do [that particular writing activity] on, but the things we're doing, we would do anyhow. I think this is just a new dimension.

Others agreed. Bev stressed that her goals did not change.

> The other thing I wanted to say is my goals are always the same. [The children] have to be happy no matter what. If being on the computer made them unhappy, then forget it.

Margaret concurred. When asked if she saw any differences in her expectations or goals for her children when they were writing using the computers, she explained:

> Basically they're the same. . . . We're worried about the capitals, we're worried about the punctuation, that sort of thing, and I'm doing the same thing with the computer that I was without it. So that really hasn't changed that much.

Initially, word processing was used in service of existing goals and in ways that were consistent with existing assumptions. Although word processing did alter the surface structure of practice, these alterations did not initially challenge the assumptions or "deep structure" underlying that practice. In time, however, the teachers came to question and critique some of their own taken-for-granted curriculum practices and to alter both their practices and the assumptions underlying those practices. (See Chapter 7 for a full discussion of this.)

However, the introduction of word processing unquestionably required that the teachers invest considerable time and effort in devising methods for the introduction of word processing skills, the instruction of those skills, and the assessment of progress. Rather than being perceived as a change, in that it represented "added curriculum" like the mandated health and handwriting curricula, this curriculum work was perceived as a means to an end. The following conversation took place in October between Debby and Margaret and was typical of many discussions in which the additional time and energy was acknowledged but considered to be justified by the outcomes.

> DEBBY: I know word processing is not supposed to be added to our cur-
> riculum, but until the children know what they're doing, it's added.
> And teaching word processing might take a little extra time.
> MARGARET: And it'll pay off in the long run because they'll be able to do
> a lot in their writing without you taking the time [away from other
> teaching responsibilities].

The teachers acknowledged that teaching word processing was at first a "burden," but they carried on because of their conviction that it would eventually help them achieve their goals. Debby explained: "The long-term benefits of it are obvious to you. [But] I can see [that] in the beginning it will be work." A month later, she complained not of the time that teaching word processing was taking away from the rest of the curriculum, but of the rest of the curriculum limiting the time for using word processing.

> I wish that all I had to be teaching right now was word processing be-
> cause I love it and I'm really excited and the amount of enthusiasm among
> the kids is something you can't put a lid on, but I have to.

The difference between the teachers' work with word processing and their work with curricula they perceived as a "change" or "added on" lay in the purposes the curriculum served. Introducing word processing instruction into their tightly packed schedules was seen as a temporary inconvenience that would eventually help children reach what the teachers held to be important goals such as positive self-concepts, independence, and an enjoyment of writing. Added curriculum that did not help children reach such goals, was regarded as "curriculum change."

The teachers' introduction of word processing into their teaching resulted in their altering, refining, and adding to their teaching, but because they were engaged in changing their teaching from year to year, week to week, and moment to moment, their overall perception of this experience was one of continuity. Furthermore, although these alterations and refinements repre-sented discontinuity in specific practice, they were consistent with the teach-ers' fundamental goals and beliefs about teaching, learning, and children, and maintained the philosophic coherence of their curricula, they were therefore perceived positively.

SUMMARY

The teachers assumed curriculum to be a dynamic construction negotiated in the day-to-day interactions of individual teachers and their children. Curriculum was assumed to be a malleable yet always coherent whole. They assumed that the knowledge that should be brought to bear on the processes of curriculum making was practical rather than theoretical, situated rather than generalized, and grounded in personal ideology and experience. Continuous change was assumed within their conception of curriculum and curriculum knowledge. Implicit in the teachers' assumptions about the nature of curriculum, the nature and genesis of curriculum knowledge, and the nature of curriculum change was the agency of teachers as creators, adaptors, and critics.

The teachers' conceptions of curriculum and their curriculum work within their classroom were sometimes consonant with, but more often in conflict with, the dominant ideologies in the surrounding contexts. In Chapter 5, three critical points of ideological conflict and consonance are identified.

5 Contexts of Curriculum Work: Conflict and Consonance

The teachers' curriculum work was set within contexts that reached back into personal and organizational histories; across the settings in which it was embedded—the school district, the school building, and the teachers' ongoing practices; and down into the underlying assumptions that formed the ideologies of the school district, the school, and the research project, as well as the personal ideologies of the teachers in their own classrooms. Together, they formed a complex and intricately woven fabric. In some places, where the histories, practices, and ideologies of many individuals came together, the fabric was dense and complex. In others, it was woven loosely and simply, its threads crossing only at distant and uneven intervals. Whether the mesh was close and fine or more coarse and open, it was durable and strong. But the fabric was never complete—its patterns and textures were continuously changing; it was always a work in progress. As will be seen in Part III, changes in the fabric of the teachers' curriculum work more closely resembled subtle elaborations of existing designs and textures achieved by picking up or dropping threads than gross alterations achieved by ripping out or patching over.

At some points, histories, practices, and ideologies were consonant. More often, however, they clashed. When seen through the teachers' eyes, the most critical conflicts were ideological. Disagreements centered on assumptions about the nature and sources of curriculum knowledge and curriculum change and about teachers' roles in the creation of curriculum knowledge and the conduct of curriculum change. At points of conflict, expectations and values clashed. Teachers' efforts were blocked, plans sacrificed, goals compromised, and energies diffused. At points of consonance, the teachers' work at least proceeded unencumbered and, in some cases, it proceeded with multiple sources of support.

Two of the three examples that follow illustrate points at which histories, ideologies, and practices converged and resulted in conflict as the teachers engaged as active agents in curriculum work. The first describes the introduction of the school district's new writing curriculum and represents recurring conflicts surrounding mandated standardized curricula. The second describes the first word-processing workshop conducted by the researchers and is representative of conflicts over conceptions of curriculum knowledge and teachers' roles in the creation and acquisition of curriculum knowledge. The third example illustrates a critical point of consonance in which the histories, ideologies, and practices of the school district, the school, the research project, and the teachers converged in support of the teachers' work as active agents in the creation and critique of word-processing curricula.

CONFLICT: MANDATED STANDARDIZED WRITING CURRICULUM

The standardized writing curriculum was introduced in the school district during the first year of the teachers' work with word processing. Several years prior to the implementation of the new writing curriculum, a committee comprised of curriculum administrators and teacher representatives was convened by the chief curriculum administrator and charged with the responsibility of selecting or creating a writing curriculum for all teachers and children in the school district. Historically, writing instruction varied across classrooms in quantity, content, and approach. While some teachers had not taught writing at all, others had taught writing in conjunction with and in response to content taught in other curriculum areas, and still others had developed separate creative writing curricula. The new curriculum differed from previous practice in that it formalized writing as a separate curriculum area, mandated particular content and strategies that were characterized as a "process approach," and monitored the quantity and quality of instruction to be provided by requiring writing samples to be submitted periodically to school principals. Over the course of the first year of the research project, all of the teachers in the school district were given instruction in the content and methods of the new writing curriculum and were expected to begin implementing it in their classrooms.

The beliefs that guided and gave meaning to the administration's move toward uniformity and accountability were clearly in conflict with those that undergirded the school's ethos and the work of the individual teachers. In the face of the changes in school district ideology, policy, and practice, the school held closely to its own history and ideology in which individual curriculum innovation and expertise were supported and rewarded. The teachers, too, held to their own beliefs and practices and to their role as active agents in curriculum matters. The three strands of ideology and practice—of school district, school, and individual teacher—converged in multiple points of conflict over both the content of the mandated curriculum and the process by which it was implemented.

Content of the Curriculum

A districtwide initiative to expand and enrich the teaching of writing might, on the surface, appear to be consonant with the school's collective efforts to develop their children's oral and written language skills. So, too, might the prescription of a process approach to teaching writing seem in accord with the teachers' considerable interest, training, and experience in using process approaches to writing instruction in their classrooms. However, the very existence of mandated standardized curricula was experienced by the teachers as a denial of their individuality, an interruption or obstacle to their ongoing curriculum work, and an affront to their existing practice and curriculum knowledge.

Conflicting ideologies. The primary conflict was not one of purpose, but of ideology. The school district assumed that high-quality writing instruction could be achieved by identifying the content and methods developed by curriculum experts and proven to be successful in other settings, training teachers to duplicate that content and those methods, then mandating their use in all classrooms. By requiring a standardized writing curriculum, the school district administration sought to assure its school board and community that every child would receive high-quality writing instruction. Quality and accountability were the goals, and uniformity of content and method were assumed to be the best means of attaining them.

The school was equally committed to providing writing instruction of the highest quality. The school district administration and the faculty of the school were in agreement that a process approach to teaching writing was a promising means of attaining that goal. Multiple points of conflict remained, however. The teachers' assumptions of the centrality of teacher individuality and teacher initiative in curriculum matters were inconsistent with the assumptions underlying both the form of the standardized, prescribed curriculum and the passive, functionary role it assumed for teachers. There was a fundamental ideological conflict over the nature of curriculum as well. The teachers based their practice on the assumption that curriculum was fluid and infinitely revisable. Because it reflected the particular context in which it evolved, it could not be set out entirely in advance. The standardized, prescribed writing curriculum, however, was based on the assumption that curriculum was a product created in advance of implementation; its generalizability was based on the assumption of fundamental similarities in children, teachers, and classroom cultures.

Barbara's response to the mandated writing curriculum illustrates the multiple sources of ideological conflict. In Barbara's case, discontent stemmed from a mismatch between her personal, professional assumptions about the individual variability of children and teachers and the role that children's perceptions of themselves as learners played in their learning and the assumptions implicit in the standardized writing curriculum. To Barbara, the standardized curriculum, by its very presumption of uniformity, was inconsistent with her own beliefs about individual variability and her intimate knowledge of the diverse needs and strengths of her children. In order to implement the standardized writing curriculum in ways that would achieve the uniformity of instruction intended, she would have to deny her knowledge of her individual children. Instead, she negotiated her writing curriculum within the bounds of the conflicting ideologies, managing rather than resolving (Lampert, 1985) the contradictions between them.

Conflicting practice. The content and methods of the mandated writing curriculum were also discontinuous with the surface features of teachers' ongoing practice. The mandated writing curriculum was therefore perceived as an interruption or unnecessary addition to the teachers' ongoing curriculum.

The degree of discontinuity varied by individual teacher. For each teacher, however, conflict centered on the fact that the standardized writing curriculum formalized and decontextualized writing. Bev, who had informally incorporated beginning writing experiences into her developmental kindergarten program, felt a separate and formal writing curriculum represented a radical departure in content and method from her previous practice. Margaret, who had previously shaped writing assignments to support and extend her reading curriculum, found that isolating writing as a separate curriculum area divorced it from meaningful content to write about. Writing, she explained, had always been an

> integral part of the reading/language arts program. We've never really had a separate writing [curriculum]. If we go on a trip, or we have a special occasion, or we're making a book, then we do separate writing, not related to our reading. But the bulk [of our writing] was related to our reading book.

Declaring writing a separate content area, with a separate time allotment and prescribed writing topics, represented a significant departure from Margaret's ongoing practice.

For Debby, the use of peer conferences in the mandated writing curriculum represented an extension and validation of her uses of peer teaching and helping. But other aspects of the mandated curriculum were discontinuous with her current practice. For example, Debby embedded writing instruction in meaningful tasks, for example, teaching the conventions of writing formal letters in the context of composing real letters. The mandated writing curriculum, in contrast, separated instruction in specific writing skills from the tasks to which they would be applied.

Consequently, the new writing curriculum was experienced by the teachers as an interference or, at best, an unnecessary addition to the content or methods that were currently part of their curriculum. As such, the requirements of the writing curriculum were treated as a collection of duties to be executed as quickly as possible. In a journal entry, one teacher wrote:

> Anyway, our new big writing project is to make our own books! Now that all the . . . required projects are out of the way, we can do what we want!

Once required tasks were completed and ideological conflicts managed, the teachers turned their attention to curriculum that they felt was more appropriate for their children and more consistent with their beliefs and practices.

Meanings. Conflicts of ideology and practice not only engaged the teachers' attention and energies, but were endowed with significance that transcended the conflicts themselves. The very existence of a mandated standardized writing curriculum, designed to replace their own existing writing curricula, was perceived as an affront to and an indictment of the teachers' established curricula and their own curriculum knowledge on which their practices were based.

The teachers fought the implication that their situated, personal, and practical knowledge of teaching and children was less valid than the theoretical knowledge of the experts who created or selected writing curriculum. They argued that curriculum experts could not know their children as they did, nor could curriculum guides address their children's various and evolving needs and strengths. Referring to a school district curriculum guide, Margaret explained: "THAT book does NOT deal with every child that comes down the road!" Only the classroom teacher, they insisted, has access to the requisite knowledge. By proclaiming their own situated, personal knowledge of children and context to be essential and inaccessible to the "experts," the teachers resisted the implication that their curriculum knowledge was inferior.

Yet the implication of inferiority was persistent. Because district-mandated curriculum was sanctioned by those in authority, it gained worth by that association. For example, one teacher referred to her own rich, ongoing writing curriculum as "my little writing projects" and to the activities prescribed by the school district as "real writing" and "formal writing projects." More often, however, the teachers responded with anger or frustration to the implication that the content of their curriculum was less worthy than that which was mandated.

Implementation of the Curriculum

Not only was the content of the standardized writing curriculum incompatible with the teachers' ideologies and practices, so too was the process by which it was implemented. The conflicting histories and ideologies of the individuals and organizations involved accounted for much of the discord.

Conflicting histories. In the year preceding the implementation of the standardized writing curriculum, all teachers were required to attend monthly training workshops conducted by the administrators and teachers who served on the language arts committee. Teachers were assigned to groups by the grade level they taught and on the basis of having had "some" or "no" experience teaching writing. Once grouped in this manner, all of the teachers in a group were instructed in the same content and in the same manner. These procedures failed to take into account the great variation in individual teachers' histories of interest in process approaches to writing instruction and the knowledge and skill they had accumulated over the years. Such procedures also failed to acknowledge the teachers' long-standing practice of "inservicing themselves." Conflict resulted when histories of teacher agency converged with present policies.

Several years prior to the adoption of the new writing curriculum, teachers in the school had begun attending, on their own initiative, workshops and college courses on process approaches to teaching writing. Many had since implemented in their own classrooms what they had learned. Margaret described the interest and involvement in process approaches to teaching writing of many of the teachers in her school

> We've been using this writing process for years and years. . . . We went to workshops on it five and six years ago, and we have always used it as an integral part of the reading/language arts program.

Knowledge acquired by teachers who had attended the workshops spread through the faculty informally and in after-school workshops held in their classrooms.

Consequently, the districtwide inservice workshops were considered by the teachers to be unnecessary in light of their accumulated knowledge and experience with process approaches to teaching writing. One teacher described the inservice meetings in this way:

> Most of what we've had at the writing workshops, we already had at workshops we've had [in the school]. . . . There are some activities that are interesting—that are a little bit different. But basically, as far as the

whole writing process goes, and what people are doing, and what people are just starting to do, we've already been doing [it] here.

Furthermore, the lack of recognition of the teachers' previous knowledge and experience was deeply felt.

Conflicting ideologies. Conflicts over practices were merely the manifestation of more far-reaching ideological conflicts on which school, school district, and individual teacher's practices were based. Underlying the conflict surrounding the implementation of the standardized curriculum were assumptions about the nature, genesis, and acquisition of curriculum knowledge, and teachers' roles in relation to curriculum and curriculum knowledge.

The teachers' assumption that curriculum is context-dependent, malleable, and generated out of the personal, practical, and situated knowledge of the individual classroom teacher placed teachers in the active and central roles of creators and implementors of curriculum. In contrast, the school district's prevailing assumption that curriculum is static, generalizable, and created and certified by experts denied the existence and value of the teachers' existing curriculum and curriculum knowledge. It precluded the kinds of engagement with curriculum the teachers had come to assume in their own classrooms by denying them opportunities to select or create, test, critique, and, when deemed appropriate, reject curriculum.

Furthermore, in the ideological contexts of the school and the individual teachers' classrooms, curriculum knowledge was assumed to be a personal construction generated by teachers in interaction with children and peers. In such a belief system, the notion of transmission or delivery of curriculum knowledge had little meaning. The role of others in teachers' acquisition of curriculum knowledge could be better described as that of bearers of personal and situated understandings offered to teachers for consideration. The proffered knowledge was meant to be grappled with, adapted, or rejected according to the particular needs of the receiver, rather than accepted and implemented without question. This conception of the process by which the curriculum knowledge of one person enters into the thinking of another person bears a striking resemblance to the conception of collaboration and colleagiality put forward by Bateson (1990) in her analysis of women's ongoing construction of their lives. This conception of learning from colleagues is based on an assumption of and respect for difference and assymmetry without dominance and on relationships characterized by interdependence rather than hierarchy established by the possession or lack of knowledge.

This relationship of knower to knowledge and knower to learner differs dramatically from that which underlies the practice of "inservicing" teachers in the content and methods of standardized curriculum. Whereas the teachers' shared ideology assumed a central and complex role for teachers in the creation and acquisition of curriculum knowledge, the traditional inservice training they received cast them in a limited and passive relationship to knowledge that was the antithesis of the agency they assumed. Within the teachers' ideologies, curriculum learning that took place outside their own classrooms was situated in collegial relations of interdependence and mutual respect. In contrast, traditional approaches to inservice curriculum training located curriculum learning in hierarchical relationships.

Summary

A striking theme in the teachers' responses to both the content and implementation of the mandated writing curriculum was their perception that their existing curriculum and the curriculum knowledge they currently held was assumed by the school district administration to be inferior to that of curriculum experts. Their indignation and assertions of superior knowledge and practice existed alongside their expressions of self-doubt. Bev, for whom the implementation of mandated standardized curriculum represented the greatest alteration in role and relationship to curriculum, expressed the sentiments of her colleagues in a whispered comment at the end of a rather heated discussion of the mandated curriculum. "I just wish they wouldn't give this to me," she said quietly as her colleagues nodded agreement.

CONFLICT: LEARNING TO USE WORD PROCESSING

The researchers planned the first summer workshop unaware of the significance of the histories, ideologies, and practices surrounding the teachers' engagement with new curriculum knowledge. The teachers' response to the structure and content after the first day of the workshop was immediate and powerful. The conflict was primarily ideological. It centered on the discrepancy between the teachers' and researchers' assumptions about the genesis of curriculum knowledge, about how teachers acquire curriculum knowledge, and about curriculum change.

Conflicting Ideologies

The researchers based their work on the conviction that the teachers, with their prior experience with curriculum and extensive knowledge of their particular context and children, were most capable of generating knowledge of how to teach children to manage the hardware and software, and knowledge of the potentials of word processing as a tool for teaching writing. Yet while the researchers espoused and acted on the belief that the teachers would acquire the subtle and complex knowledge required to teach word processing and to use word processing in their teaching through their own explorations and experimentation, the acquisition of the much simpler skills of how to manage the word-processing system seemed to be regarded differently. The design of the workshop suggested that the only way the teachers would acquire this knowledge was by direct instruction. The researchers had predetermined what word-processing skills the teachers would need to know, when they would need to know them, and how they would best be acquired.

The teachers, however, disagreed. They assumed that knowledge of what word-processing skills they would need to learn would be determined in their deliberations about their goals for word processing use and by their knowledge of their existing curriculum, their classroom context, and the needs and strengths of their children. Therefore, the word processing skills the teachers would need to learn could not be determined by anyone other than themselves. Furthermore, the teachers assumed an active role for themselves in the acquisition of this knowledge, not the passive role of receiver of direct instruction. The teachers had a long history as learners as well as the conviction that continuous learning about curriculum was a fundamental part of teaching. In the past, some teachers had elected to learn in formal programs of study offered by the school district or by universities. Others sought ideas and information from colleagues, journals, and their own experimentation in their classrooms. Their learning was ongoing and, in all cases, initiated and structured by the teachers themselves in response to their own interests or needs. It was this conception of themselves as active agents in their own curriculum learning that the teacher brought to the initial word-processing workshop.

An additional source of conflict was the inclusion of activities designed to engage teachers in their own writing. The researchers' decision to focus on writing as well as word processing was based, in part, on the assumption that the introduction of word processing into their classrooms would necessitate the rethinking of the teachers' existing ways of teaching writing. The teachers, it has been seen, did not regard the introduction of a new writing tool as an occasion to alter their current teaching practices. To the contrary, they regarded it as a time to protect the integrity of their ongoing curriculum in order to explore word processing from a stable base of established practice.

Two excerpts from field notes made early in the second day of the workshop recount the events, but do not capture the full measure of frustration felt by both the teachers and the researchers. The first excerpt identifies the presenting problem—the inclusion of writing exercises in the previous day's agenda. The second provides a sample of the ways in which the deeper conflict over the possession of valid curriculum knowledge was voiced.

> [One teacher] brought up concerns that she and another [teacher] had discussed last night. They were feeling that they didn't need to learn the writing process—that they already know how to teach this.

Although the teachers' perception that the researchers did not acknowledge their expertise as teachers of writing was the focal issue, the scope of the discussion that followed quickly expanded to include word processing and classroom logistics as well. Underlying this discussion were conflicting assumptions about the genesis and ownership of valid knowledge about teaching and learning in the teachers' classrooms.

> [The teachers] expressed many logistical concerns. . . . About two full hours of discussion of problems that they anticipated included:
> - problems with parents whose children were not being taught to use word processing
> - problems with colleagues who would be disturbed by the noise of the printers in the open-space classrooms
> - problems because the second and fourth grades each drew children from all classes in the grade level to form their language arts group. Would they have to teach all children in the grade level [to use word processing] as well as all the children in their reading groups AND their homeroom groups?

For each problem enumerated, the researchers offered suggestions, but none proved satisfactory. In each case, the teachers cited conditions specific to their own classrooms that made the proffered suggestions unworkable. By refuting the researchers' proposals, the teachers used their knowledge of their particular classrooms to establish that they, not the researchers, had the critical knowledge about how word processing would work in their classrooms.

The teachers and researchers had conflicting assumptions about the determination of the knowledge the teachers would need to begin to teach with word processing and the manner in which they would acquire that knowledge. Although some of the most basic word-processing skills the teachers would need to know could probably have been determined by anyone who had used word processing, only the teachers could know what other procedures would be of use. For example, basic word-processing procedures, such as indenting and centering, that the researchers had planned to teach were not immediately necessary for some of the teachers. These procedures could be learned when they became necessary in their work with the children. They wanted to know, instead, how to program the printer to produce primary type and print labels. These were far more complex procedures, but the teachers believed they could enhance their teaching, and they therefore wanted to learn them at the outset.

Moving Toward Consonance

By the end of the second day of the workshop, the researchers altered their plans for the remaining sessions. Individual exploration of the capabilities of word processing replaced directed learning tasks. Researchers were available to answer teachers' questions as they arose about the computer hardware and word-processing software rather than to instruct the teachers in their use. The teachers determined, from an array of capabilities, which word-processing procedures they would need to know. Teachers and researchers thought aloud together about how the children might approach the technology, what kinds of instruction might be most appropriate, what kinds of support might be necessary to permit them to work independently at the machines, how the limited number of computers would be shared by a full class of children, the relative merits of children working alone or in pairs at a computer, and the kinds of writing tasks that would be most appropriate. The teachers assumed their accustomed role as active agents, exploring and creating their own knowledge of both the capabilities and management of the hardware and software, their understanding of how their students might approach it, and its potential for advancing their curriculum goals.

When the teachers were supported in their roles as active agents in their own acquisition and creation of knowledge rather than impeded, their learning proceeded rapidly and without conflict. Each teacher determined what, how, and when she would learn according to her own current level of expertise, interest, curriculum goals, and the needs and skills of her children. Not surprisingly, the teachers varied as widely in the style, content, and pace of their learning as did the children they taught.

Bev, for example, cautiously sought the support and coaching of her husband, who had extensive computer experience. Barbara, in contrast, proceeded essentially on her own. She was described by a colleague as spending

> . . . 78 hours on the computer! . . . non-stop! . . . [she] came up for breath [and said to me] "I need to know this and this and this. Can you come help?" . . . then right back!

Barbara talked informally with others who had used word processing to learn what its capabilities were, then explored the software on her own at home. When she reached problems she could not solve on her own or with the manuals, she sought answers from other teachers or researchers. Debby spent two summer afternoons with a colleague to be taught "like I was one of the children," then spent time on her own exploring and practicing. She confessed to "dreaming about computers!" saying, "That's the way I get when I'm learning something new. . . . This is really invigorating!" Margaret's approach to learning word processing required time on her own to wrestle with procedures. She described her deliberate approach to learning how to print labels.

> Even though Jessica [the researcher] would have been able to tell me the spacing without [my] having [had] to work it through, I will remember much better how to do it by having figured it out by myself. For me, working things out by trial and error on the computer is better than having someone tell me what to do—I never remember when I have to do it on my own if someone just tells me.

No predetermined or uniform approach to helping these teachers learn to use word processing could accommodate their wide range of differences in needs and styles. Furthermore, no directed learning situation could have been consonant with the teachers' collective beliefs in their agency as learners of as well as creators and critics of curriculum. Only when the researchers began to create and re-create their workshop plans in interaction with the teachers and the content in this particular historical and ideological context was conflict diminished and consonance of ideology and practice approached.

Summary

The initial workshop plans did not recognize the teachers' need to maintain the integrity of their ongoing curriculum during the initial stages of introducing word processing or take into account the teachers' prior knowledge of computers, word processing, and writing, nor did they acknowledge the teachers as active agents in the acquisition and production of curriculum knowledge. The teachers were addressed as receivers of knowledge held by the researchers rather than owners, creators, and critics of their own curriculum knowledge. The researchers did respect the teachers' knowledge of teaching and learning and the teachers' privileged knowledge of their own contexts, and in fact had planned that a considerable amount of time in the week-long workshop would be devoted to the teachers talking about their general curriculum goals and practices and their goals and plans for using word processing in their teaching. However, the researchers' predetermination of what writing and word-processing skills the teachers would need and the manner in which those skills were presented did not acknowledge or value the teachers' prior knowledge and experience with computers and teaching writing. This contradiction was not lost on the teachers.

Over the course of the week-long workshop and throughout the first full year of the research project, the teachers and the researchers struggled to make their beliefs and practices understood by and consonant with the others'. Understanding, and the trust it engendered, did not come easily. By the second year of the study, when Barbara and Debby joined the group, the researchers had made a conscious effort to align their behavior with their espoused beliefs. The researchers planned the workshop week around the teachers' requests for specific training, discussions of their plans, and time to pose their questions to the researchers and the three veteran teachers. The teachers decided how, how much, and how quickly they would learn about the technology and which of its applications were best suited to their purposes. In the spring of the second year, when updated versions of the word processing software and a spelling checker were added, each teacher explored its capabilities in her own time and at her own pace. We continued to move haltingly and tentatively toward consonance of all of our practices and beliefs.

CONSONANCE: WORD PROCESSING

The teachers' work with word processing, on the other hand, was marked by a significant degree of consonance. A confluence of conditions and events in the school district, school, and research project supported their work in several important ways. Most significant among these were the parallel interest in word processing of the school district, school, research project, and individual teachers; the provision of the necessary hardware, software, and consumable supplies by the school district, school, and research project; and past and present (although not necessarily contemporaneous) policies of the school district, school, and research project that supported teachers' curriculum work. This unusual consonance of purpose and practice supported the teachers' agency as owners, creators, and critics of significant curriculum knowledge in their work with word processing.

This is not to say that conflict ceased to exist. It was neither cancelled out by this experience of consonance, nor could it be said that it was balanced by consonance to create a neutral state. Instead, the teachers' work with word processing proceeded within the larger contexts of contradictory beliefs about teachers' roles and relations to curriculum, curriculum knowledge, and curriculum change. Conflict and consonance existed side by side in the teachers' curriculum work.

Interest in Word Processing

Several years prior to the beginning of the research project, the school district began to support the use of computers in secondary schools. In response to requests from several teachers in West Brook Elementary School, hardware and software were made available to them as well. The faculty's initial interest in computer use in classrooms led to disillusionment. Little of the software available to them—primarily collections of drill and practice programs—supported their curriculum goals. Interest was growing among some teachers and the principal, however, in exploring the potential of word processing.

At this time, the director of the research project approached the principal and several school district administrators with a proposal to conduct research on microcomputers and children's writing development. In preparing their proposal, the researchers, too, had selected word-processing software over other language arts-related software. They based their choice on research on children's acquisition of literacy that situates literacy learning in the acts of writing and reading rather than as preparation for writing and reading (Calkins, 1983, 1986; Graves, 1983). Whereas most drill-and-practice software isolates particular skills for practice, word processing permits children to learn these same skills within meaningful texts that they themselves create.

Fortuitously, school district, school, research project, and individual teacher interest in educational uses of computers in general and word processing in particular converged in time. The result was an unusual consonance of interest as well as multiple sources of material support.

Material Support for Teacher Agency

Initial provision of computer hardware, software, and consumable supplies was made by the school district. Although hardware and software were to be installed in the secondary schools first, a particularly knowledgeable and enthusiastic teacher in the school, with the support of a central office administrator and the former principal, managed to acquire one computer for each grade-level team and a library of drill and practice software. The hardware was stored on carts and rotated through the classrooms within each grade level. The school, through the current principal's discretionary fund and donations by the Home and School Association, provided each grade-level team with additional disk drives, computer printers, and supplies of paper, disks, printer ribbons, and additional software as interest shifted from drill-and-practice software to word-processing software. The research project, through funding from IBM and Scholastic, provided each teacher in the research project with two or more computer systems as well as word-processing software. This abundance of hardware and software permitted the project teachers to conduct their work with word processing in a setting in which many of their colleagues were also engaged in explorations of computer use. Additionally, it permitted the project teachers to conduct their work at any time of day, without interruption and without being dependent on the rotation of equipment within the grade-level team.

It is important to reiterate that the teachers' and researchers' preference for word-processing software over drill-and-practice software or tutorial software was significant. Word-processing software, a tool use of computer technology (Taylor, 1980), permitted the teachers to apply it to their own goals and devise their own tasks rather than, like other software, supplying them with predetermined content, goals, and tasks. Word processing thus offered the teachers the opportunity to engage in curriculum work as active agents. However, the provision of a curricular material that provided teachers with a tool to be used in service of their curriculum work rather than a means of controlling their work (Apple, 1983) was a necessary, but not sufficient condition for agency.

Policies Supporting Teacher Agency

Past and present policies, in multiple contexts, supported the teachers' agency in their work with word processing. Some policies enabled the teachers to acquire considerable expertise in creating, critiquing, and adapting curriculum; other policies permitted them to use these skills in the present context. The period of laissez faire curriculum policy in the school district's history permitted the teachers to develop a repertoire of the skills required to create portions of their own curricula. More recently, the teachers had extensive experience adapting received curricula in response to the introduction of standardized curricula. These skills, discussed at length in Part III, were brought to bear on the tasks of selecting word processing skills to teach, determining the order in which to teach them, and selecting or devising materials, methods, and groupings for instruction.

The teachers brought to this opportunity to create their own curricula a rich history of experience initiating curriculum innovation in a school context in which curriculum initiative had been widely valued and supported. The teachers brought knowledge not only of the processes of curriculum work, but, in this case, some valuable content knowledge as well. As a result of their earlier explorations of microcomputers in their classrooms, computer technology was not entirely new to them, nor were the logistical issues surrounding managing computer use in their classrooms. Some teachers had also been acquainted with other word-processing programs. Only the particular word-processing software itself was new to them.

Supports for teacher agency were established in the design and conduct of the research project as well. Because the researchers sought to document the children's and teachers' work rather than to impose and manipulate experimental conditions, the researchers introduced no overt constraints on the teachers' choice of activities, pacing, style, sequence for instruction in, or application of, word processing. As Bev explained to Barbara when Barbara was about to join the project in its second year, "Don't feel like you're going in [to this project] and they're expecting something, because they're not." Then, laughing, Bev added, "They're not here to be leaders!"

Policy support, or more accurately, the absence of policy at the school-district level supported the teachers' agency as well. Because unresolved differences precluded agreement, no standardized computer curriculum was in place. The absence of a mandated standardized computer curriculum did not represent a shift from the school district's assumption of curriculum as a product devised by experts and handed down to teachers for implementation. It did, however, result in a condition in which teachers were free from the constraints of required materials, tasks, and timetables. In this case, the school-district policy that permitted teacher agency, in the absence of ideological support from the district for such agency, was sufficent to permit the teachers to proceed with their work with word processing. Consonance of ideology and practice between the school district and the teachers regarding curriculum work became less critical for the teachers because ideological and practical support were available in the school and the research project.

The teachers' work with word processing occurred at a point of unusual consonance of histories, policies, and practices in the school district, school, and research project that converged in a collective direction of energies and resources toward the shared goal of using word processing in the teaching of writing. Current interest and past and present policies in all contexts established conditions that supported the teachers' agency in the development of word-processing curricula.

SUMMARY

Among the critical features of the setting in which the teachers created their own word-processing curriculum were the ideological contexts of the district administrators, the researchers, the principal, and the teachers themselves. Assumptions about teachers and their roles in relation to curriculum, curriculum knowledge, and the process of curriculum change differed sharply, leading the administrators, the researchers, and the principal to act in ways that either supported or impeded the teachers' curriculum work.

Where policies, practices, and ideologies converged, the teachers' active engagement with curriculum proceeded with multiple sources of support. More often, however, the contexts in which the teachers conducted their work were characterized by conflict. It was within these multiple and often conflicting contexts that the teachers engaged in the processes of developing word-processing curricula and conducting classroom-level curriculum change.

Part III
PROCESSES

Prevailing conceptions of the processes of curriculum innovation and change neither describe nor explain the experiences of the teachers in this study as they created their own word-processing curricula and altered their existing curricula to accommodate the introduction of new content and methods to their teaching. Current models of curriculum innovation and change describe a linear sequence of discrete tasks that begin at the point of curriculum design (Miles, 1964) or at the decision to adopt a curriculum (Berman & McLaughlin, 1978; Fullan, 1982; Gianquinta, 1973; Huberman & Miles, 1984). In the implementation stage that follows, the innovation may be co-opted, adapted (Berman & McLaughlin, 1978), or transformed from its original form and intent (Fullan, 1983; Huberman & Miles, 1984), or it may fail to be implemented at all. If successful, the innovation is stabilized as teachers and administrators master its use and administration (Huberman & Miles, 1984). The process is completed when the curriculum innovation is "institutionalized" or established as a routine part of school budgeting, planning, and operations (Berman & McLaughlin, 1978; Fullan, 1982; Gianquinta, 1973). Across models, the number of stages and the names given to the stages differ, and the emphasis each model places on a particular stage varies. But the process they all describe is invariant. Curriculum materials are created or selected, the curriculum is delivered to the teachers who are required to implement it in their classrooms, and the success or failure of an innovation is gauged by measures of the extent of use and fidelity to the intended form of the innovation.

Without exception, the prevailing models are based on studies of imposed, systemwide curriculum change, and they describe and interpret curriculum work through the lenses of rationalist assumptions about curriculum and school management. Focusing the study of the process of curriculum innovation and change at the level of the institution fails to attend to any but the reactive features of teachers' work. Only behaviors construed to be related to the proposed curriculum change are noted. Consequently, prevailing models of curriculum innovation and change overlook teachers' ongoing creation and critique of curriculum in their own classrooms, and, in some cases, misinterpret that work. No model that attends only to the reactive features of teachers' curriculum work could be expected to adequately describe or explain the curriculum work that teachers initiate and direct in their own classrooms.

Basing the study and implemention of curriculum innovation on rationalist assumptions further limits the capacity of prevailing models to describe or explain the work of the teachers in this study. In these models, the separation of the role of creator of curriculum from that of implementor, and the separation of creation from implementation are assumed. The creation of curriculum knowledge is regarded as the province of curriculum experts; implementation is the responsibility of classroom teachers. In the teachers' curriculum work, however, the teachers were both creators and implementors, and the processes of curriculum creation and adoption of the new curriculum were inseparable. Each teacher created and re-created her curriculum informed by what she learned during the implementation of that curriculum. No model that attends to teachers only as faithful or resistant implementors of curriculum will uncover the full extent of the teachers' curriculum activities.

In prevailing models, the process of curriculum innovation and change is assumed to be largely uniform and predictable within and across settings. A model, then, needs only to identify, describe, and order the activities or concerns that are found in all settings. The teachers' curriculum work, however, proceeded through multiple and contemporaneous processes that were recursive and not clearly differentiated. Furthermore, the path of each teacher's curriculum work varied considerably. No model that assumes uniformity and predictability could capture the complexity and individuality of their work.

In prevailing models, the process of curriculum innovation and change is also assumed to be neatly bounded in time with clearly marked beginning and end points. In contrast, the teachers' curriculum work had no clearly marked beginnings or ends. The teachers' work with word processing was better described as an extension of their ongoing engagement in multiple and overlapping curriculum processes in which they were the principal agents. The beginnings of their work with word processing were to be found in their individual curriculum experiences and institutional histories. Closure or completion of their work did not exist. By their own definitions, their curriculum work was ongoing and always open to revision. No model that treats curriculum change as an event separate from and interjected into the teachers' day-to-day curriculum work could accurately characterize, or lead to understanding of, that work.

In Part III, an alternative frame is constructed for understanding the processes of curriculum innovation and change in which teachers are active agents. It is grounded in the teachers' experiences of, and consistent with their assumptions about, curriculum knowledge, curriculum, and their roles in relation to both and reflects the meanings the teachers ascribed to the processes of curriculum innovation and change.

6 Beginnings: Reluctance Reconsidered

In curriculum work, Grundy (1987) points out, "seldom do we start from 'scratch'" (p. 6). Teachers are engaged not only in ongoing curriculum practices at the time of curriculum innovation and change (Grundy, 1987), but they bring to the process their complex histories of engagement in past instances of curriculum change as well. In this case, the teachers brought their experiences of creating and altering their own curricula during the period of laissez faire curriculum policy in the school district and of critiquing and adapting the new standardized curriculum. These experiences represented an accumulation of goals, beliefs, and practices that shaped the teachers' ongoing curriculum as well as an accumulation of skills that enabled them to make and respond to curriculum.

In addition, the teachers' histories of curriculum experiences formed the lenses through which they perceived the process of curriculum change itself. Britton (1987) states that as continuous learners, we come to each new experience "not only with knowledge drawn from the past but also with developed tendencies to interpret in certain ways" (p. 16). Each teacher, even the youngest among them, had accumulated extensive experience with curriculum innovation and change through which they anticipated how the work with word processing might proceed and interpreted what actually transpired. Whereas traditional models locate the beginnings of curriculum innovation and change in the creation of the curriculum, it is necessary to locate the beginnings of the teachers' work with word processing in their ongoing curriculum practices and prior experiences with curriculum innovation and change.

Two themes emerged in the teachers' early work with word processing that can be understood only in light of their prior experiences. The first was the teachers' persistent requests that they be told what the researchers expected them to do with word processing. The second was the teachers' insistence that they would use word processing in ways that replicated, rather than altered, their current teaching practices. Both of these themes could be interpreted as indicators of the teachers' reluctance or inability to engage as active agents in curriculum innovation and change. The teachers' requests that the researchers tell them how they were expected to use word process-ing might be misconstrued as expressions of their inability to deal with new curricula without outside guidance. Similarly, their insistence that they would use word processing in ways that replicated their current classroom practice might be misinterpreted as conservatism or even resistance to change. However, when these responses to new curricula are set within their his-torical and ideological contexts and seen from the meaning perspectives of the teachers themselves, they represent functional responses and important antecedents to significant change rather than endpoints or signals of failed change.

"I DIDN'T KNOW WHAT I WAS SUPPOSED TO DO"

The data on the first four months of the study are replete with teachers' requests that the researchers tell them how they were expected to use word processing. Questions such as "Is this what you want?" and "What do you want me to do?" were common.

The researchers, however, had no expectations of how the teachers should use word processing beyond that they would use it in ways that they believed best supported their teaching and their children's learning of writing. This condition, to which the teachers had agreed in their decision to join the research project, was ideologically consistent with the teachers' own assump-tions about the context-specific nature of curriculum and teachers' active roles in curriculum work. Furthermore, the reseachers' ethnographic research design included no controlled conditions and no standardized measures. The teachers were required only to allow the researchers to observe and record classroom work with word processing, to be interviewed periodically about their work with word processing, and to attend monthly research meetings.

The researchers were frustrated by what they perceived as the teachers inexplicable requests for prescriptions. The teachers had repeatedly demon-strated their ability to create curricula without direction from outsiders. Fur-thermore, the teachers chafed against curriculum prescriptions imposed by the school district. The researchers groped for ways to understand. It seemed at first that the teachers' questions were indications that they doubted the researchers' sincerity and thought that the researchers had specific expecta-tions that they were withholding. The teachers' repeated requests to be told what they were expected to do with word processing might just as easily have been interpreted as their reluctance, resistance, or inability to take greater responsibility for curriculum decisions. But the explanations were neither that simple nor that clear.

"You Have to Realize What We Were Used To"

The very experiences that had prepared the teachers so well with the skills required to create and critique curriculum also made agency difficult to achieve and fraught with misunderstanding in this unusual situation. Their work with word processing differed in important ways from their prior experiences with either received curriculum or with curriculum they created themselves. First, this curriculum work was initiated outside the school district. The decision to introduce word processing had not been mandated by the administration, nor had the teachers initiated this work on their own. Instead, they had been invited to participate in an arrangement jointly negotiated by their administrators, their principal, and the researchers. Second, in the absence of a standardized computer curriculum, there was a conspicuous lack of prescribed tasks, methods, and assessments. Within a curriculum largely predetermined by others, the teachers' work with word processing was conducted in an unusual pocket of sanctioned professional discretion. Third, the teachers, for the first time in their experience, created curricula while researchers observed and documented their work.

With no analogous experiences on which to base their understanding of this work, the teachers brought "developed tendencies to interpret" (Britton, 1987, p. 16) their work with word processing in terms of their past experiences with curriculum introduced by someone other than themselves. In short, the teachers assumed that the researchers, like the school district administration, would expect that word processing should be used in specific ways in their classrooms. Consequently, they sought to clarify these expectations.

In a meeting of the research group at the beginning of the second year of the study, teachers and researchers looked back on the tension they had experienced over expectations. One teacher summarized what they had been experiencing by linking this experience to those in their collective past.

> You have to realize what we were used to . . . . We didn't know what to do when you didn't tell us what you wanted . . . when you didn't tell us what to do.

She continued, explaining that based on their past experiences with mandated curriculum, they were

> trying to figure out how to get around [the researchers' requirements for word processing use] and get on to what we wanted to do with it.

The pattern of establishing expectations, then "getting around" those expectations and "getting on to" their own curriculum work was so powerful that its disruption caused a great deal of anxiety. Recalling the beginnings of work with word processing, the teachers described the feelings associated with expecting that the researchers would tell them what to do and finding that this did not occur. When asked to recall the most difficult parts of her first year of work with word processing, Margaret explained in an interview:

> I think the worst part was not really knowing . . . what was expected, thinking something was expected when it really wasn't expected.

Bev echoed this anxiety in her first journal entry at the beginning of the second year:

> Starting off this year *knowing* [her emphasis] or understanding what the research project is all about takes away the confusion and questioning that was confronting me at the outset of last year's program. Knowing there are no limits or boundaries to the project opens the door to anything we want to do.

The need to know what was expected of them as a precondition of their curriculum work was so much a part of their prior experience, and of their interpretations of their current experience, that even assurances from colleagues that there were no expectations to fulfill did not convince them that this was the case. Even after Bev assured Barbara, as she was about to join the project in its second year, that she need not feel that the researchers were "expecting something, because they're not," Barbara sought assurance from the researchers as well. In her first formal interview, she shifted the focus of the discussion to expectations: "My question is, what do you want?" Later, in a journal entry, she reiterated: "I'm interested in knowing what you expect from us."

Although knowing what they were expected to do with received curriculum was a precondition to initiating their own work with that curriculum, it was not directives that they sought from the researchers. Margaret explained:

> I didn't know what I was supposed to do, what you expected, how much or how little . . . . I didn't know what *I wanted to do in my classroom with what you wanted to be done* [emphasis added].

Efforts to get the researchers to tell them "what to do" and what was expected of them did not so much represent requests for guidance as they did means of determining the boundaries or limits that would be placed on their curriculum work. They were seeking not prescriptions but parameters within which they could conduct their work.

Parameters vs. Prescriptions

Looking back on her first year of work with word processing, Margaret recalled:

> Now I realize that you wanted us to do whatever we wanted to do and that was fine. I really didn't understand that at all. I expected a list of expectations—what the kids would be doing and that type of thing.

Although they expected a prescriptive list of curriculum activities or requirements, it was clear that they did not need or want such a list. The teachers referred with disapproval to such requirements placed on teachers who had participated in other research projects. Margaret continued:

> They had certain things they had to do . . . four things that all of the children had [to have] done on the computer by the end of the year. And we had none of that, which is better because it's silly to have [the children] sit down and type in their name, type in a sentence. This way they had the computer a lot more and they typed in their name every time they sat down to type.

Such requirements, in light of the teachers' experiences as participants in a research project and creators of word-processing curricula, seemed both simplistic and unnecessary.

Yet at the beginning of the research project, prior experience with curriculum making led the teachers to seek out the very types of expectations that they shunned. Perceived from the teachers' perspectives, their actions were informed by, and in keeping with, their past experiences with curriculum change. Their questioning and persistent search for the limits that they assumed would be placed on their work were artifacts of these past experiences with curriculum. They were expressions of the teachers' very realistic need to know the parameters within which they could proceed, or what they must "get around" in order to "get on to" their own uses of word processing.

Basing expectations of current curriculum work on past experience might be understood by some as a failure of imagination or an inability to conceive of the possibilities to be found in more empowered relations to curriculum. However, there may be wisdom in interpreting current curriculum work, at least in part, using prior curriculum experiences in the same context. For although the teachers' work with word processing differed in significant ways from their prior curriculum work, it took place within the same historical and ideological contexts and was therefore subject to many of the same influences. For the teachers to enter into a situation that supported or encouraged teacher agency in curriculum matters with expectations that did not take into account these historical and ideological contexts would have been naive, at best. Rather than a display of reluctance to engage actively in curriculum innovation and change, their behaviors reflected their personal, situated knowledge of the context within which they would conduct that work.

"MORE OF THE SAME"

Just as the teachers' quest for what was expected of them could have been misinterpreted, so, too, might their plans for their initial uses of word processing have been misconstrued as indicators of conservatism or reluctance to change. In every case, the teachers made it clear that the uses they made of word processing would not alter but would reinforce their established curriculum practices and goals. Barbara's plans for using word processing are illustrative.

> The ways I plan to use the computer as a tool in my classroom will have pretty much to do with the kind of things that I have done in the past.

Margaret described her initial uses of word processing in similar terms.

> Basically [the children] do the same . . . I'm doing the same sort of thing with the computer that I was without it.

In no case did the teachers look on the introduction of word processing, a tool that required skills and offered possibilities unlike any other in their curricula, as an occasion to alter their established curricula or to reflect on the goals, assumptions, or conduct of their practice.

On the surface, the teachers' talk of using word processing to replicate rather than alter their current curricula resembled that of teachers (often described as "conservative") who subsume curriculum innovations into their ongoing curricula in ways that produce not change but "more of the same" (Lortie, 1975). Such perceptions of the teachers' initial work could be troubling to advocates of word processing or process approaches to writing who see in word processing technology opportunities to highlight the malleability of text and to encourage response and critique by peers, and to those who see curriculum change in general, or the introduction of technology in particular, as a stimulus to reflection on practice and professional growth. Although the introduction of word processing offered the opportunity for significant changes in thinking and in established practice, the possibility remained that computers would be employed as nothing more than very expensive typewriters to meet the goals, and replicate the existing strategies, of teaching writing with pencil and paper. However, the teachers' uses of word processing, which appeared to co-opt word processing in the service of ongoing practice, in fact, formed the foundations of the significant changes that were to come.

Too often consideration of instances of curriculum change and other educational innovations have ignored the phenomenology of that work (Fullan, 1982). Failure to account for the meaning perspectives of the participants, according to Fullan, lies at the heart of much failed educational change. In this instance, failure to understand the teachers' tenacious defense of their ongoing practice from their perspective could too easily lead to unfair attributions of foot-dragging conservatism or premature pronouncement of the introduction of word processing as a failed innovation. In order to understand the beginnings of the teachers' work with word processing, it is necessary to take into account their assumption that curriculum is to be maintained as a philosophically coherent whole.

Maintaining Integrity of Existing Curriculum

In Chapter 4, the teachers' assumption of curriculum as a coherent whole was established and a distinction was made between changes in the surface of curriculum and changes in its deep structure (Bussis, Chittenden, & Amarel, 1976). The case was made that the coherence or integrity of a teacher's curriculum was to be found in its deep structure. Although introducing word processing required, at the very least, the addition of new content—teaching children how to use the technology—and the creation of scheduling strategies for sharing two to four computers among more than 25 children, surface changes in the teachers' practice were kept to a minimum and the deep structure, or the teachers' fundamental goals and beliefs, initially remained unchallenged.

Margaret, for example, organized her morning instruction around her meetings with her reading groups and planned to fit her uses of word processing into this existing organization. Within this structure she had no time to spend at the computers with the children. The children in Margaret's class first used word processing with the help of a university intern and one of the researchers. Her decisions about which children should use the computers, and when they would use them, were based on the existing reading group structure. The researcher working with Margaret noted in her log:

[Margaret] has orchestrated the [children's] turns at the computer so that [they] fit her reading group [schedule]—I was never working with a child who should have been in a reading group.

One reading group at a time was introduced to word processing. When Margaret felt the children were capable of working at the computers without adult supervision, she designed writing tasks that were structured enough to allow them to proceed without calling her away from her work with the reading groups (Kahn, 1988).

In addition to maintaining the integrity of her daily schedule, Margaret developed uses of word processing that were consistent with, and did not challenge, the content of her reading and language arts curricula. Children were taught the word-processing capabilities needed to produce and manipulate texts in ways that paralleled their writing with paper and pencil. They were taught to enter texts using lowercase and capital letters, to delete letters and words, and to correct simple errors in spelling and word choice. Word-processing procedures that would allow the children to revise the meaning of their texts, like moving and inserting text, were not taught initially because Margaret believed the children would not need them. She explained,

> You see, they really don't [change] that much. At that age, they are happy with what they wrote down first and they don't want to change it.

Her initial uses of word processing were shaped to be consistent with the surface structure of her ongoing practice, and therefore did not disrupt her teaching or challenge—at least at first—her assumptions about children, teaching, and learning.

Barbara also framed her plans for word processing so that they were consistent with her ongoing practice.

> I have thought of times in my schedule that I could set aside [and] ways to schedule kids [so that] they could experiment and do all that kind of thing. Using the computer as a tool in my classroom will very much have to do with the kind of things that I have done in the past.

Barbara initially used word processing to record the children's dictation and print out their dictated sentences and stories to be bound in class books. Furthermore, as has been seen, Barbara would not consider any use of word processing that was not in keeping with her assumption of the centrality of a positive self-concept.

Even Debby, who modeled her initial plans to introduce word processing on the procedures used by veteran teachers, soon altered her plans to more closely match her own established practice of encouraging children to teach other children. In an early journal entry, she wrote:

> I have made up my mind that I will introduce it to the whole group and use the aid of the large keyboards I have made for the kids. We will

> practice manually at our desks before I take them to the actual computer.
> . . . After a week of mini-lessons I have prepared in which each of the
> children will practice typing in [his or her] name, a short sentence, [and
> so on], we will be ready to use the computer for our own writing.

But these plans were not consistent with her current practice of sharing the
teaching role with her children. In these plans she was the source of all knowledge and skill, when, in fact, she valued the children's teaching and helping
each other. She had explained in an interview that preceded this journal entry
that she believed her own role was "not being the instructor in the class all
the time." The discrepancy between her plans based on other teachers' procedures and her own goals and current practice was too great. She soon abandoned her initial plans in favor of practices that more closely matched her
own values and her established teaching practices.

> I am using the kids who know the [shift key and space bar] as my first
> set of computer experts! They are really excited. There are 12 of them,
> so I'm pairing them up with the 12 who don't know [those keys]. They
> will be going to the computers together for a while.

Olson (1988) suggests that teachers use existing routines to cope with
the novel demands of an innovation in order to maintain control over their
teaching. He describes such behaviors as "protective strategies" that maintain the "core elements" of their work so that they can meet curriculum
expectations while maintaining smoothly functioning classrooms and fulfill
responsibilities to children, colleagues, and administrators. Whereas in an auto-
mobile factory production is shut down while machinery is retooled and workers retrained to alter production, making curriculum alterations is neither as
simple nor as mechanical. Teachers cannot be removed from classrooms and
retrained in the content, materials, and methods of a new curriculum, although
prevailing models of curriculum implementation assume this is appropriate.
Teachers' true engagement with new curricula takes place in interaction with
their children in classrooms that are in full operation. While teachers explore
and learn new content and methods, students continue to require teachers'
full attention as they grow and change, and administrators and parents continue to expect positive results.

Cuban (1986), in his analysis of teachers' uses of classroom technology,
suggests that "stability in teaching practice and the craft of instruction are
positive forces in schools, maintaining a delicate balance amidst swiftly changing public expectations" (p. 7), as well as an appropriate response to the
multiple and conflicting curriculum demands placed on teachers. He con-
cludes that, given the conficting expectations of teachers and the limited re-

sources available to them, modest, incremental changes in largely stable curriculum and teaching practices should be valued. The teachers in this study were indeed working in a context characterized by multiple and conflicting curriculum expectations. But the findings in this study suggest that the modest changes made in surface curriculum to accommodate word processing use should be valued, not necessarily as end points or as the limits of what might be expected, but as the critical foundations on which later and more significant changes were based.

Co-opting vs. Establishing Foundations

Using a curriculum innovation to replicate, support, or extend existing practices and goals can be viewed as building a stable foundation on which to base curriculum development and change or as co-opting the innovation. Studies of curriculum implementation have frequently characterized teachers' initial incorporation of an innovation into their ongoing practice as co-optation—using the innovation in the service of existing purposes and procedures. In cases identified as co-optation, teachers were reported to adopt only those parts of an innovation that were consistent with their current practice or to alter the essential nature of the innovation in some way to make it consistent with existing practice (McLaughlin, 1976). The introduction of "process approaches to science" (by the American Association for the Advancement of Science and the Science Curriculum Improvement Study, for example) in the 1960s and 1970s illustrated this process. Teachers who were accustomed to teaching science as the transmission of facts used the activity-based materials to teach, and test children's acquisition of, facts rather than to engage students in active exploration and discovery and in the development of science process skills. In studies of this and other instances of imposed curriculum change, teachers' initial assimilation of new materials or methods into their current practices has been considered a problem to be overcome or an early sign of a failed innovation.

The teachers' initial uses of word processing, described previously, resembled co-optation in critical ways. The teachers were clearly using word processing to meet their existing goals in the teaching of writing and to reinforce their existing activities and methods of instruction. Even the addition of new content—the teaching of word-processing skills—was accomplished within existing structures for scheduling and grouping for instruction. The teachers' work with word processing differed from co-optation, however, in that it was not an end point but a starting point.

Stenhouse (in Rudduck & Hopkins, 1985) advises teachers to accept "the curriculum and teaching you are now engaged in as a starting point" (p. 86) of all curriculum work. Grounding their initial teaching strategies for and uses of word processing in their current practice permitted the teachers to begin exploring word processing without compromising the smooth functioning and coherence of their existing curricula. Furthermore, in using word processing to reinforce existing practices lay the seeds of the significant change to follow.

Barbara's initial decision to use word processing as a tool to quickly and efficiently record her children's dictation is illustrative. Barbara perceived word processing as offering the potential to allow her children, many of whom found printing a laborious task fraught with errors, to produce perfectly formed letters in invariant left-to-right order and spaced and positioned correctly on lines. However, she and the researchers assumed the technical difficulties of managing the word-processing system would lead the children to experience more failures than successes. Barbara's decision to send each child to the computer with an adult to record his or her dictation not only supported her existing goal of providing multiple opportunities for her children to see printed text as "talk written down," but also solved the problem of the perceived mechanical complexity of managing the technology. Within one of Barbara's existing practices—recording children's dictated stories—lay the seeds of significant change in her practice.

For each of the children sitting next to the adult at the computer, the lure of the keyboard that invites a child to touch, the appeal of a tool associated with adults, as well as the ease with which it produced letters on the screen proved irresistible. It became clear that it was neither possible nor desirable to exclude the children from participating in recording their own words. Dictation gave way to a new writing event—collaborative writing. Each child was encouraged to participate by typing familiar words or letters, holding down the shift key, pressing the space bar, or adding a period (on cue from the adult) while the adult performed all the rest of the word-processing tasks. Over time, as the children gained in writing and word processing skill, collaborative writing evolved into coached writing. The children shifted their chairs in front of the keyboards, nudging adults into the peripheral role of providing occasional assistance with word-processing procedures or writing skills. Both collaborative and coached writing represented significant change in the existing writing instruction in Barbara's classroom. Out of the existing practice of recording children's dictation a new context for learning to write had been developed in which each child enjoyed the full attention of an adult who collaborated with the child on the production of his or her text. (See Cochran-Smith et al., 1991 for a fuller description of the evolution of collaborative and coached writing.)

In his treatment of the introduction of computers into human thought and activity, Weizenbaum (1976) notes that

> To say that the computer was initially used mainly to do things pretty much as they had always been done, except to do them more rapidly or, by some criteria,

more efficiently, is not to distinguish it from other tools. Only rarely, if indeed ever, are a tool and an altogether original job to do invented together. (p. 32)

Similarly, the teachers, in their ongoing invention of their writing and word-processing curricula, did not ask what new curriculum work they could perform with the tool of word processing, but rather, how they could use it to enhance their current work. Weizenbaum develops the argument that it is in this very enhancement of existing work that such work may be opened to examination and the possibility of substantive change. "It may seem odd," he continues, "even paradoxical, that the enhancement of a technique may expose its weaknesses and limitations" (p. 35).

This was indeed true of the teachers' work. Margaret, for example, used word processing to enhance her teaching of letter- and word-level editing. Doing so revealed the children's interest in and ability to make meaning-level revisions, thereby challenging her assumption that second-grade children are happy with what they write and are not interested in changing it. Until the introduction of word processing, Margaret's practice of limiting instruction to letter- and word-level editing was based on all the evidence available to her prior to the use of word processing. The evidence—numerous observations of the children's reluctance to make changes to laboriously handwritten texts, compounded by the occurrence of new errors in the recopied texts— was compelling. When making corrections with word processing, however, some children added words, phrases, or sentences as well, demonstrating interest and capabilities that had previously been masked by the difficulties they experienced in rubbing out, squeezing letters and words into unyielding spaces, and recopying corrected paper-and-pencil texts (Cochran-Smith et al., 1991). This new evidence, uncovered in the use of word processing to support the existing practice of teaching letter- and word-level editing, led Margaret to alter her assumptions about her children's ability to rework texts and to adapt her writing instruction.

Similarly, when writing with word processing freed Bev's children from the burden of laboriously drawing individual letters, their abilities to compose and encode texts was unmasked. Bev initially planned to use word processing in much the same way as she did many of the materials in her classroom—as a tool for children to experiment with and explore. She planned to allow the children to 'play" at the computer during their free choice times. Their play primarily involved trying out individual keys or combinations of keys and watching the effects their actions produced on the screen.

However, early in the school year, children playing at the computers displayed considerable skill and interest in copying words displayed in the classroom and reproducing known words and names from memory. Some children even tried composing sentences and brief stories using familiar words and invented spellings. Encouraged by their demonstration of skill and enthusiasm for writing, Bev reconsidered her prior practice of delaying phonics instruction until January and began instruction in phonics in the late fall.

Although the beginnings of the teachers' work with word processing initially reinforced existing goals and practices they, in fact, served as the foundations of a longer process that eventually led to rethinking and changing practice. When grounding new curriculum work in existing practice is viewed as the foundation rather than the failure of curriculum development, the question becomes not how to prevent teachers from neutralizing innovations by subsuming them into their existing practice, but how to support teachers' initial work with an innovation in ways that take advantage of opportunities for curriculum improvement and professional growth. However, a note of clarification and caution is necessary. While grounding new curriculum work in current practice may maintain the integrity of that practice without precluding significant change to follow, it does not guarantee it. The possibility still remains that the curriculum innovation will be used in ways that merely replicate what has gone before without engaging the teacher in reflection, critique, alteration, or reinforcement of existing practice.

RELUCTANCE, RESISTANCE, AND AGENCY

In this chapter and in the previous chapter, three frequently maligned and misinterpreted teacher responses to curriculum change have been identified. The teachers' claims during the summer workshop that using word processing would not be possible in their classrooms; their insistence that the researchers tell them what they were to do with word processing; and their plans to use word processing to replicate existing practice resembled what might be interpreted as reluctance or inability to change. These responses to curriculum innovation and change resemble behaviors that have led to the characterization of teachers as "stone-age obstructionists" (Doyle & Ponder, 1977) or as demonstrating "knee-jerk conservatism" (Cuban, 1986). Yet when set within the complex historical and ideological contexts the same behaviors may be understood as functional responses to the immediate and past realities of those contexts.

When seen through the experiences and ideologies of the teachers themselves, acting as agents of curriculum development and change within their own classrooms, these behaviors can be understood not only as accommodations to realities in the contexts that shaped their work, but also as a form of quiet resistance to the forces in those contexts that denied, limited, or threatened their agency in curriculum matters. Their resistance differs, however, from the critical resistance examined by Stone (1988) on two important points.

First, whereas Stone identifies resistance as a public, political act, the teachers' resistance was decidedly private. The teachers' discussions of their strategies for circumventing the mandated standardized curriculum emphasized their efforts to avoid drawing attention to their strategies. As one teacher explained, they may meet the goals of the standardized curriculum by significantly altering its form, but, as she repeated, "You don't tell them that." Second, whereas critical resistance is a political act aimed at transforming an inherently unequal and unjust distribution of power and responsibility (Stone, 1988), the teachers' resistance was directed inward rather than outward with the aim of maintaining opportunities to initiate, create, and critique curriculum knowledge and to act on their assumptions about the coherent, practical, personal, and contextualized nature of curriculum within their own classrooms. Theirs was a quiet form of resistance designed to withstand external threats to their agency rather than to confront and transform them.

The teachers' quiet resistance, although it sometimes resembled reluctance to change their curricula, was therefore a characteristic, and a means, of maintaining their agency in curriculum matters. In a context dominated by ideology and practice that disempowered teachers in their relationships to curriculum, these three instances of apparent reluctance to alter curriculum can be interpreted instead as the teachers' continuation of their ongoing critique and questioning of curriculum and their assertions, and defense, of their agency in curriculum matters. A reconsideration of the teachers' responses to the researchers' plans to devote the summer workshop to direct instruction in word-processing skills and exercises in writing, described in Chapter 5, suggests that they were direct responses to researchers' plans that left their knowledge of curriculum and context unacknowledged, and precluded their initiative to acquire and create curriculum knowledge. The teachers' claims that word processing "won't work here" indicated not foot-dragging conservatism or recalcitrance, but an assertion of their extensive knowledge of their own curricula and contexts and an effort to communicate the essential and superior nature of that situated, practical knowledge. Only they knew the way sound carried in their open-space classrooms, the intricacies of forming and scheduling reading groups within a grade-level team, and the possible responses of parents in their community to the children's access or lack of access to word processing.

Similarly, the teachers' requests for the researchers to "Tell us what you want us to do" may be understood not only as a pragmatic response in an historical and ideological context that carefully delineated their curriculum work, but also as a search for the limits within which they could conduct their work as agents of curriculum making and critique. Seen in this light, knowledge of what they were expected to do was a precondition of agency.

These instances not only serve as examples of the teachers' agency, but also highlight the limits of their agency in this setting. It is significant that their resistance was reactive rather than proactive. The teachers set out to determine the limits of their discretion and then react within those parameters. They were not given the opportunity to participate in setting those parameters. They were not participants in weighing the relative merits of and establishing the curricular goals within the school district. Nor were the teachers included in the consideration of alternate ways of addressing the issue of accountability or the consequences of dealing with accountability by standardizing curriculum. Questions of the maintenance of separately defined curriculum areas, the processes of evaluating and revising curriculum, and introducing the new curriculum to teachers and children were beyond the limits of their agency. The boundaries within which they exercised agency were tightly drawn. Within these boundaries lay decisions about how to meet mandated curriculum goals and opportunities to devise curricula to meet the personal goals they set for their children. Outside these boundaries lay participation in consideration of the most basic curriculum questions of what aims were to be pursued and what content was most appropriate as the means of reaching those aims.

Finally, reconsideration of the teachers' insistence that "I'm not doing anything I didn't do before" suggests that, rather than unwillingness to change, their initial work represented adherence to their own assumption that the integrity of the deep structure of the curriculum must be maintained. Their assumptions about the importance of philosophic and pragmatic coherence and wholeness of curriculum precluded immediate and sweeping changes in their practice, yet formed the foundations of the significant changes that would follow.

When seen from the perspective of teachers acting as agents in curriculum work, responses that may be misconstrued by others as teachers' reluctance to alter their curriculum and teaching are understood as expressions of quiet resistance to threats to their agency. They are demonstrations of, or defenses of, their empowered relationships to curriculum and curriculum knowledge and their active roles in curriculum innovation and change.

SUMMARY

The beginnings of the teachers' work with word processing were found to be deeply rooted in the historical and ideological contexts of their curriculum work. Their prior experiences with curriculum built expectations of how curriculum change initiated by someone other than themselves would proceed. It was through the lenses of these prior experiences that they conducted and ascribed meaning to their initial work with word processing. As their work with word processing progressed, their funds of accumulated experiences with the process of curriculum innovation and change were altered. So, too, were their perceptions and expectations.

Viewed through the lenses of the teachers' prior experiences and expectations, the teachers' behaviors that might be interpreted as demonstrating that teachers do not have the requisite skills to create their own curriculum, or the desire to alter their existing curriculum, may in fact be seen as functional responses to the historical and ideological contexts and as the foundations on which successful curriculum work can be built. The influence of the teachers' past and ongoing curriculum work on their perceptions of the process of curriculum change was not static, however. Once their work with word processing was under way, their initial explorations of the content to be taught, and the context in which they would conduct their work, were added to and influenced their ways of working and seeing their curriculum work. Just as the relationship between the teachers' work with word processing and the contexts in which they conducted that work were interdependent and compounded over time (see the introduction to Part II), so, too, were their experiences with the process of curriculum innovation and change, and the lenses of accumulated experiences through which they interpreted the processes in which they were engaged.

Regarding the teachers' initial work with word processing as the foundation of later work frames teachers' work with curriculum as a developmental process in which early activities and concerns are qualitatively different from those that follow and from the eventual outcomes of such work. Without benefit of knowledge of the teachers' past experiences and expectations, it would have been easy to conclude that they were incapable of or unwilling to engage actively in curriculum innovation and change. When seen in historical context, the teachers' reactions can be understood as responses to a particular context and as foundations of work to come.

7 "Just Experimenting": The Processes and Progress of Curriculum Work

If the teachers had merely assimilated word processing into their ongoing practice, the impact of this curriculum work would have been limited to minor surface changes in the equipment used for, and the management routines of, their teaching. The goals, content, and nature of the learning activities that characterized their writing instruction would have remained substantially unchanged. However, this was not the case. Each teacher not only added a new writing tool, she also challenged and revised her existing writing curriculum to reflect what she learned about her children, writing, learning, and teaching in the course of her work with word processing.

Several teachers characterized the means by which they accomplished this work as "just experimenting." The teachers' individual and ongoing experimentation, however, was carefully reasoned and represented a form of "purposeful engagement" (Dewey, 1916) and the "conscious, interested and committed" involvement in a task (Greene, 1978b) that make significant changes in thinking and practice possible. It exemplified Britton's (1987) conception of teaching as "inquiry, . . . discovery, a quiet form of research" (p. 15). The teachers, to varying degrees, all questioned the appropriateness and effectiveness of their individual goals, content, materials, and methods. Each teacher examined the impact of her ways of teaching word processing and uses of word processing on her children and on other parts of her curriculum. Any content or practice that was deemed inappropriate or ineffective was altered or abandoned. Like Stenhouse (in Rudduck & Hopkins, 1985), who characterized curriculum as hypothesis, the teachers treated their goals, content, materials, and methods as tentative answers to their questions about what word-processing skills were of most value to teach, when and to whom they should be taught, what methods of instruction were most appropriate, and in what ways word processing might be used most effectively and appropriately in their teaching of writing. In doing so, the teachers not only generated word-processing curricula that were effective and responsive to their children's needs, they also confronted, questioned, and, in many cases, altered their practice and their thinking about teaching word processing and writing.

Yet, one teacher, who described her early work with word processing as "experimenting or whatever," used the term *experiment* apologetically to mean what one does when one doesn't know what else to do. Another teacher, who described her initial work as "fiddl[ing] around with" word processing, expressed the wish that a researcher had not been present at the beginning of the year because she would have preferred to conduct these explorations without being observed. Both of the teachers' characterizations of their inquiries into teaching writing with word processing make light of their experimentations and explorations rather than accept them as legitimate ways of coming to know.

It is not surprising, however, that the teachers spoke of their work in such terms. Prevailing positivist conceptions of curriculum making characterize this work as a systematic, linear, sequential process based on the presumption of knowledge of what content and methods are most appropriate and effective. The teachers' work did not approximate the neatly predictable, scientific, rational process of curriculum creation and implementation that is associated with legitimate curriculum making. The teachers engaged, instead, in multiple, simultaneous, and continuous curriculum processes and moved through and among these processes in a recursive and episodic fashion. If measured against prevailing conceptions of curriculum processes that are neatly labeled, ordered, and bounded in time, the teachers' work may have seemed disorderly and even random or unfocused. However, to speak of their experimentation in terms that diminish it denies its significance to the course of their curriculum work and to their own agency.

This chapter begins with a description of the processes by which the teachers moved from the foundation of existing ideologies and ongoing curriculum practices to the examination and significant change of beliefs and practices. Then, the nonlinear, nonsequential progress of their work is examined. Finally, a frame for understanding and describing the teachers' work as active agents in the creation and critique of curriculum is offered as an alternative to prevailing models of curriculum innovation and change.

THE PROCESSES OF CURRICULUM WORK

Three ways of engaging in the creation of word-processing curricula were common to all of the teachers. Each questioned the effectiveness and appropriateness of the curriculum she created, observed her children's interactions with it, and altered it. None of these processes—questioning, observing, and altering—was new to the teachers. Each teacher had a history of engaging in questioning, observing, and altering curriculum mandated by the school district and curriculum that they created themselves in the contexts of their own classrooms.

Although each process is described separately here for the purposes of exposition and analysis, no single curriculum process stood entirely alone. Questioning and observing most often occurred in tandem. Questioning and observing were sometimes the basis for altering curriculum practice or thinking about curriculum, but on other occasions, altering some aspect of the curriculum prompted questioning and observing. As will be seen, events cited as examples of one process invariably include elements of the others.

Questioning

Questioning was at the heart of the teachers' work with curriculum. Each teacher posed questions in response to the unique issues raised by any new curriculum and to the issues with which she was currently grappling in other parts of her teaching. Because curriculum was assumed to be a coherent whole, the teachers did not focus their questions narrowly on word processing, but considered word processing as it interacted with and influenced other related parts of their curricula. Questions were posed, as well, about the claims made by computer experts and advocates about the advantages of word processing. Barbara, for example, approached word processing with questions about claims that the novelty of the computer might generate enthusiasm for writing in some children. She wondered if this novelty would be sufficient to motivate her children to overcome their reluctance to write.

> I'm not really sure what will happen when you add that magical tool, the computer, which they all love. I'm really not sure [that they will be] less inhibited.

The teachers also posed questions that reflected their concerns about the possible detrimental effects of word processing on beginning writers. Throughout the first year of her work with word processing, Bev grappled with her questions about the possibility that the time her children spent writing with computers might interfere with their progress in writing with pencil and paper.

> Although they've enjoyed [word processing]—it's been fun—is this too early [for them to be introduced to it]? Should they really be . . . getting that pencil in the hand and making those letters?

Definitive answers were not necessarily reached. Instead, tentative answers prompted further questions.

Although expressed in the form of skepticism and doubt, the teachers' questions did not so much reject the notion of introducing word processing into their teaching as represent the teachers' entry into thoughtful engagement with it. Their questions about word processing served not to obstruct or preclude change, but to initiate cycles of questioning, observing, and altering their curriculum practice and thinking about curriculum. Both the forms and the purposes of their questioning bear closer examination.

Questioning to gather data. The teachers routinely posed questions to gather data on which to base their curriculum goals and activities, and to assess the impact of word processing on their curricula, their daily routines, and their children's development as writers and as users of word processing.

Bev' s first explorations of word processing were guided by her question: What can five-year-olds do with a computer?

> I came saying, "Hey, let's try it." Look at it for the first few weeks. Have [the children] over [at the computers], and try to see what would go on there.

Similarly, Margaret's decision to observe her children's reactions to the complex computer keyboard rather than labeling the necessary keys and masking others over, as some of her colleagues had considered doing, was guided by her question of how her children would respond to the complexity of the keyboard.

> I don't want to do anything yet. I want to wait until they use it a little bit to decide whether to use [stickers on the keys] or not. . . . I want to try it without [stickers] just to see how they do. I thought in the beginning they would use [function keys that they did not need] and that I'd have to keep them covered up with different stickers and I would like to try it without them and see what happens.

Information gathered as a result of these questions and observations provided a firm base on which both Bev and Margaret based subsequent practice. Bev found that her children were interested in and capable of locating and pressing the keys necessary to type out familiar names and other known words, and she subsequently provided time and encouragement for them to do so. Margaret found that the large number of special function keys on the keyboard did not distract her children and that they quickly became adept at locating the keys that they needed. She proceeded with word-processing instruction without masking or labeling any keys on the keyboard.

Questioning to critique. The teachers questioned not only to gather information about their children and the technology on which to base their curriculum, but to critique existing curriculum, newly mandated curriculum, and curriculum they were creating for their own classrooms. As described earlier, Debby questioned the appropriateness of some elements of the mandated writing curriculum. For example, based on her observations of her children and her knowledge of teaching writing, she critiqued and found wanting the prescribed practice of isolating prewriting, drafting, revising, editing, and publishing from composing real texts, and altered her instruction to allow her children to learn those skills while engaged in their own writing projects.

Debby, like her colleagues, questioned and critiqued curriculum she created herself with equal thought and energy. For example, she questioned the effectiveness of her strategy of pairing novice computer users with slightly more experienced peers to receive coaching in and assistance with word-processing skills. This practice appeared to be effective, but, as she explained in a journal entry,

> Since [using] the computers in my classroom [is] such an independent task for the children, I really am not aware of the progress each of them is making as an individual. So I decided to take a survey.

She posed 16 questions to the class about their proficiency in word processing. Then, questioning the accuracy of the information she gathered in this group interview, she planned opportunities to verify and extend what she had learned about their skills. She did so by rotating responsibility for loading the computers each morning before school among pairs of students. As she worked with each pair, she observed and talked with the children about their knowledge of word processing. What she learned pleased her.

> Two designated kids [came] to the computer to boot, retrieve, edit, save, print, and clear. So far, so good. . . . [Even] the kids I didn't think knew very much did manage all the above skills with me watching.

Having identified the children who had not yet mastered the skills she had specified as necessary, Debby coached each child in the skills he or she was lacking.

The teachers' questions guided their active engagement in their study and critique of the potentials and liabilities of word processing in their classrooms. Although some questions led to overt action, like Debby's survey, this was not always the case. Many of the teachers' questions, like Bev's and Margaret's cited above, led to observation—an activity often so subtle that it might be assumed that there was no engagement with curriculum at all. Yet observing was central to the teachers' curriculum work.

Observing

In the examples above, the teachers' questions were related to and dependent upon their observations of their children and of their own practice. Observing provided answers to questions and also prompted questions. An example from Barbara's work illustrates the interdependence of questioning and observing in the teachers' work.

Interdependence of observing and questioning. Barbara observed that her children were beginning to write formula sentences at the computer. She marveled at their skill and wanted to know more about the conditions that led to their success. She began by questioning whether her children were composing the formula sentences on their own or whether the fourth grade student who assisted in the afternoons was supplying these patterns. Barbara discussed her thinking in an interview shortly after she had observed this work.

> I really don't know how it happened. Is [the helper] that much of a natural [teacher] or are the kids hooking into one of the patterns? I have tried very carefully to develop patterns—"I am thankful for ___ ," or whatever, and they can type the whole next line themselves. . . . But then I noticed that [the helper] was taking dictation from them and that they would produce things like "I like duh, duh, duh. I like duh, duh, duh." So one day I thought, "Well, I'm going to stand here and watch this," because it was everything [I was aiming for]—and I had never discussed it [with them]! The kids WERE picking it up. The KIDS were the ones that picked up the pattern. They would start it. . . . They would do four or five [sentences] and then they would switch the pattern and continue.

Observation led Barbara to the question, "How did the children come to compose formula sentences?" Her question led her to further observation. Both observing and questioning yielded critiques of the effectiveness of the use of formula sentences in previous paper-and-pencil writing activities and of the practice of allowing children to go to the computer to write on topics of their own choice with the support of an older student-volunteer. These practices also yielded valuable information about her children's skills and confidence as beginning writers.

Observing and questioning were so much a part of Barbara's work with word processing that she kept a small notebook at the computer in which she entered daily notes about individual children's activities at the computers. For example, she recorded:

> Sung put spaces between his names. Used all lowercase letters. Then the word "room." Where did he get that? Then "107": "sung ho room 107." [I] asked him how he knew how to spell room—no reply!

Further consideration led to the speculation that he had memorized the words and numerals on the sign displayed at child's-eye level outside the classroom door. Barbara's observations of Sung, and others who copied text from labels throughout the classroom, lent credence to this hypothesis and suggested that copying labels and other words displayed in the classroom may have possibilities as a planned use of word processing in her curriculum.

Observing and questioning to generate curriculum knowledge. Through the ongoing interplay of questioning and observing each teacher increased her knowledge of how her children learned word-processing skills, and how they learned to compose, revise, and edit their writing with word processing. Each teacher built a fund of curriculum knowledge of what goals and content were reasonable and appropriate, and what instructional materials and applications of word processing were effective. At times, increased knowledge led to the validation of goals, materials, or methods. More often, however, it led to changes in the goals, content, instructional methods, or organizational structures surrounding the teachers' writing instruction.

Altering

Alterations were made both to the surface features of the teachers' practice—the ways they organized time, space, grouping for instruction, and the actual learning activities they engaged in with their children—and to the goals and accummulating curriculum knowledge underlying that practice.

Altering curriculum practice. The teachers undertook the process of altering curriculum practice with seriousness and purpose. No alterations recorded in the data were made without the direction and supporting evidence provided by their questions and observations. Margaret's journal entry following her first word-processing activity is illustrative. It demonstrates the ways in which alterations to her methods for introducing the children to some of the capabilities of word processing and for providing initial instruction in several basic skills such as spacing and capitalization were grounded in the data she had accumulated on her children, her teaching, and her view of the computer as an object of instruction.

> [The] children were very interested in the computer the first day so I decided to try using it with the whole group. They would dictate a few

sentences about something special they did over the summer. I would type it into the computer and print it out. Disaster! Twenty children could not see the screen or printer or wait for a turn. The next day [the university-student teaching assistant] took the rest of the children individually and typed in their dictated stories, then printed them.

After observing that her children expressed interest in the computer on the first day of school, she altered her day's plan to include a first experience with the computer. Observing that the small screen and the position of the printer did not allow children to follow her demonstration, and that the children, eager to share their sentences and have them entered and printed out, were having a difficult time waiting patiently for their turns, she altered her plans once again. Her new plans provided each child with an opportunity to dictate sentences to an adult and observe the adult enter the sentences on the keyboard, to locate and use the keys for spacing, capitalization, and punctuation, and to follow the procedure to print his or her sentences.

In the extended example below, we look again at excerpts from Debby's journal that demonstrate the purposefulness of the teachers' alterations and the role observation and questioning played in this process.

9-5-86   I have made up my mind that I will introduce [word processing] to the whole group and use the aid of the large keyboards I have made for the kids. We will practice manually at our desks before I take them to the actual computer. . . . After a week of [the] mini-lessons I have prepared in which each of the children will practice typing in their name, a short sentence, [and so on], we will be ready to use the computer for our own writing.

9-23-86   I am experiencing a little frustration dealing with the fact that some of them ready to roll and others are not. . . . Plan B—The computer experts will be shown as a separate group how to save and retrieve. . . . They will be at the computer both helping the others and producing work of their own on a disk. Lessons they will help the beginners with will be as simple as:
1. typing a simple sentence
2. typing a short poem
3. typing in a short letter

10-2-86   I've had a major change of thought! So what else is new? I found out that the beginner computer kids were extremely bored with typing in stuff that was not meaningful to them. And seeing their expert pal type in his or her own story really bugged them. So, they are now also typing in their first story. . . . They seem to be a lot slower but their pals are real nice at coaching them through.

The alterations Debby made were significant. Her observations of her children's frustration with touch-typing instruction led her to reconsider one of her initial goals—to teach the children to be proficient typists before they began to write with word processing. Debby's observations of her children's responses to full-group instruction also yielded information on the variation among her children in their familiarity with the keyboard. Based on this information, Debby abandoned full-group instruction in keyboarding and created expert-novice pairs. Her initial plan to provide word-processing instruction in the context of structured writing exercises was also called into question when she observed that her children were bored by writing tasks that had no real purpose or audience.

Altering curriculum knowledge. Just as questioning and observing were associated with alterations in practice, so were they associated with alterations in the curriculum knowledge that underlay practice. The teachers' explorations of the hardware and software extended their content knowledge or mastery of word-processing skills. Observing and questioning as their children wrote with word processing challenged, supported, or extended their curricular knowledge, or knowledge of the capabilities of word processing as a tool for teaching writing, as well as their pedagogical content knowledge or knowledge of how to create learning experiences to extend their children's abilities to compose texts and master word-processing skills. For example, Margaret's knowledge of the potential and limitations of word processing as an object of or tool for full-group instruction was extended, confirmed, or challenged through questioning and observing. Both Bev and Margaret refined their knowledge of the limitations of word processing as a tool in full-group dictation on the basis of their questions and observations of their children's interest and involvement in these activities.

Knowledge of the sequence and timing of instruction in word-processing skills based on their own experiences learning word processing—that basic typing facility should precede instruction in cursor movement, movement between screens, and load, print, and save procedures—was altered through the processes of observing and questioning their children's early work. Similarly, several teachers who, as competent writers and typists, experienced learning word processing as a complex task held that word-processing instruction should precede, and be entirely separate from, writing instruction on computers. This knowledge was altered as a result of the teachers' observations and questions, which led them to create learning activities in which their children learned word-processing skills in the context of their own writing projects.

In similar fashion, knowledge of the range and relative value of various strategies for teaching children to perform the procedure to print their texts was increased, revised, or elaborated. Also, knowledge of procedures to provide assistance to children who needed help with a word-processing problem while the teacher was involved with other children was replaced, refined, or extended.

The teachers' inquiry surrounding the creation of word-processing curricula enabled them to see and re-see the word-processing curricula they were creating, and to see their own established curriculum and the knowledge underlying their practice in light of this new element in their curriculum. Teachers engaged in such intentional inquiry are known to revise their own practice on the basis of their questions and observations (Bissex & Bullock, 1987; Duckworth, 1986; Mohr & MacLlean, 1987; Tikunoff and Mergendoller, 1983). The processes of observing, questioning, and making successive alterations were the mechanisms by which the teachers moved away from their initial uses of word processing that had replicated ongoing curricula in goals, assumptions, and procedures. In the following section, the interplay among these processes and the teachers' ongoing curricula are examined more closely to determine how they were related to both the creation of effective word-processing curricula and the critique and modification of the existing curricula into which word processing was introduced. In order to understand the ways in which questioning, observing, and making alterations drove curriculum thinking and practice, it is necessary to look back at the conception of curriculum knowledge that underlay the teachers' work.

Inquiry, Curriculum Knowledge, and Curriculum Change

The conception of curriculum knowledge on which the teachers based their practice was one of personal and practical knowledge situated in time as well as place. Knowledge of what content was necessary and appropriate and how to create and conduct learning activities that enabled children to acquire that content was assumed to be generated and tested in the context of teachers' and children's interactions with content in a particular classroom, and at a particular time in their history together. The processes by which the teachers acquired curriculum knowledge were questioning, observing, and making informed alterations to their curricula.

Because the processes of questioning, observing, and altering were ongoing, the teachers were sensitive to the inevitable changes that took place within a class of children over a school year and the differences between one year's class and the next. They were also sensitive to the incremental changes that took place in their own understandings and knowledge of word processing and how to teach children to use word processing, as well as in their knowledge of children's writing development in general and their own children's writing development in particular. The teachers' ongoing engagement in questioning, observing, and altering their curricula yielded a body of curriculum knowledge that shifted and grew as the experiences of the teachers and children grew and changed. The curriculum knowledge on which the teachers based their curriculum practice was, as Polanyi (1969) asserts all knowledge is, "always on the move" (p. 132).

Figure 7.1 illustrates the relationship between the teachers' existing curriculum and practice and the ongoing processes of questioning, observing, and altering them. The periphery of the figure represents the individual teacher's interrelated processes of questioning, observing, and altering curriculum. At the center is the focus of these curriculum processes—the individual teacher's current curriculum knowledge and curriculum practices. At any given point in time, one or more of the goals, materials, or methods of the teacher's existing curriculum, of a newly mandated curriculum, or of a curriculum she is creating in her own classroom may be the focus of observation, questioning, or alteration. In the teachers' curriculum work, instances of engagement with the new or existing curriculum began with one of the three processes and proceeded along any of several paths. In some cases, it began by the teacher's observing existing practices, questioning their effectiveness, then altering those practices. In other cases, it began instead with a teacher's question and proceeded to her observing and then further questioning or alteration. In the case of mandated curriculum change, required alterations to a teacher's existing curriculum led to questioning and observing, which was often followed by alteration of the mandated curricula.

Figure 7.1 *Relationships between individual teachers' curriculum knowledge and practice and the processes of questioning, observing, and altering curriculum*

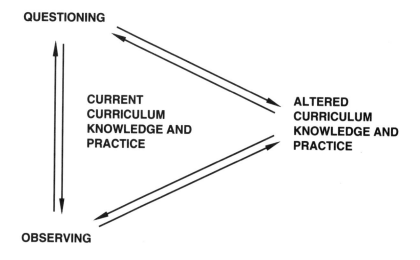

Each successive question, observation, or alteration to the curriculum took place in a context that differed from the contexts in which previous curriculum deliberations had taken place. Once a teacher observed, questioned, and perhaps altered a particular word-processing activity or instructional practice, that experience yielded curriculum knowledge on which subsequent curriculum deliberations would be based. Furthermore, each new goal, material, or method became part of the context of ongoing practice in which new or existing elements of the curricula were created or critiqued. Consequently, subsequent alterations to curriculum were questioned and observed in a context of ongoing practice and curriculum knowledge that differed from those surrounding earlier decisions. Curriculum practices created at one point in time were observed and critiqued in a context of different curriculum knowledge and ongoing practices than those created earlier, and practices that once proved effective might be deemed less so when judged in a context of new practices and understandings. Curriculum that was questioned and observed in changing contexts did not remain static.

An example from Margaret's early word-processing work demonstrates the ways in which questions, observations, and alterations to an initial use of word processing in her curriculum moved her word-processing curriculum away from replication of existing goals, content, and methods and significantly altered her teaching of writing. At the outset, word processing was assimilated into her existing ways of teaching children to edit their writing. When teaching children to edit their paper-and-pencil writing, Margaret sat with a child or small group of children and made corrections in spelling, punctuation, and capitalization on each of their compositions. Producing an error-free final product required that each child then return alone to his or her desk to laboriously produce a corrected copy by hand. Margaret's practice reflected her assumption, supported by her observations of her children's reluctance to correct or even acknowledge errors in their laboriously handwritten texts, that second graders were incapable of finding and correcting their own spelling and punctuation errors.

Margaret replicated her goals and methods of teaching editing with pencil and paper when she first introduced her children to word processing. She, or an adult assistant, sat with a child or a pair of children at the computer and located the errors that required correction. The task—editing a piece of writing—remained the same. However, the tool used to record and edit the piece had been altered. When word processing was inserted into this existing practice, Margaret's observations yielded information that led her to question her assumptions about her children as writers.

When her children worked with an adult to edit their work at the computer, they demonstrated that, in fact, they could find some of the errors in their own texts as well as in those of their partners. In some cases, the children were even eager to find and erase errors and insert corrections. With this new information about the children's willingness and ability to find errors in their writing, Margaret altered her goals, expectations, and procedures for editing their writing. Subsequently, Margaret and pairs of children worked together to locate errors in the printouts of both children's rough drafts. The pair of children then returned to the computer to make all of the corrections without adult supervision. The author of the first text sat at the computer. His or her partner held the printout, showed the author where the next error was indicated, and assisted in locating the necessary keys and printing out the final copy. When the first text was corrected, the children changed places and repeated the procedure.

The effects of observing, questioning, and altering her practice were significant. Surface changes to Margaret's procedures for editing texts fundamentally altered the social context surrounding learning to edit in her classroom. Rather than learning to edit by watching an adult make corrections to their texts and then recopying corrected texts on their own, children and adults sought errors together, and children assisted children in making the necessary corrections. The deep structure of her practice was also challenged as she questioned and altered her prior assumption that second-grade children were not willing or able to find and make corrections in their work.

To this point, the progress of the teachers' work has been described as though it moved inexorably forward over time. This was not the case. Inquiry, creation, and critique of curriculum did not proceed linearly or at a steady pace.

THE PROGRESS OF CURRICULUM WORK

Existing models of curriculum making and curriculum change identify a linear sequence of discrete activities that follow one another in invariant order and are to be completed in a predetermined period of time. The curriculum-making activities in which the teachers engaged were not clearly delineated. Setting goals and creating materials and activities, implementing them, and evaluating the outcomes were not discrete activities in the teachers' curriculum work and therefore these labels have little descriptive or analytic power. Nor was the teachers' progress through curriculum making linear, determined, or bounded in time; their progress is better characterized as recursive and episodic movement through the interdependent processes of observing, questioning, and altering curriculum.

Curriculum Work: Recursive vs. Linear

Questioning, observing, and altering, like the processes of scientific inquiry that they resemble, are by their very nature related in a recursive rather than a linear manner. As demonstrated in the examples provided above, questioning and altering were followed by observation which was followed, more often than not, by further questioning or alteration. The overall effect was one of interdependent processes looping back on themselves in varying order.

In addition, the teachers' progress was recursive in the sense that they returned again and again to particular questions. Questions were rarely answered definitively when they were first asked. Because of the ever-shifting nature of the context of the teachers' curriculum work, some questions that seemed to be answered satisfactorily at one point in time might be asked again in light of later practices and curriculum knowledge. More often, the questions asked were neither simple nor direct and required consideration from many perspectives and through the lenses of many acccumulated experiences.

The teachers' recurring questions concerned the goals they had established for their word-processing curricula, the content they had selected to teach, and the methods and materials they devised. For example, Bev's recurring concern over the possible impact of word processing on her children's efforts to learn to print, which was referred to earlier, was captured in two questions—"Would composing at the computer interfere with early efforts to learn to write with pencils and paper?" and "Would seeing only capital letters on the keyboard impede their learning to recognize and use lowercase letters in their paper-and-pencil writing?" Both questions recurred, without resolution, throughout the first two years of Bev's work with word processing. Excerpts from field notes and interviews document the recurence of these questions:

> *2–86 Fieldnotes*   Bev pointed out that she noticed that [when the children were using pencil and paper] they were beginning to write their names in lowercase letters but that when they wrote other words, they did so in caps. She suggested that this was because they were using the computer [and that] the keys were in caps.

> *2-86 Interview*   Oh, something else I thought of. A lot of them have had great difficulty in getting their name down to lowercase letters. . . . They write in capitals.

> *6-86 Interview*   You know, I talked to you about this, that now they seem to be writing in capitals and they're not getting lowercase letters in. . . . and it's crossed my mind, although they've enjoyed [word processing]— it's been fun—but is this too early [for them to be learning this]? Should

they really be working with the tool of getting that pencil in the hand and making those letters?

2-87 Interview I still think about the idea. You know my feelings about the [hand] writing. I don't know if [word processing] interferes.

That Bev did not arrive at definitive answers to her questions does not diminish their importance. Each round of questioning and observing led her to consider and reconsider continuing or altering her current allotments of time for writing with word processing and writing with pencil and paper, and maintaining or altering her emphasis on using lowercase letters. Each time she returned to grapple with these questions, she did so against a backdrop of greater experience and accumulated knowledge about her children's development as writers with both pencils and computers.

Bev also returned again and again to questions about the use of dictated stories in her teaching of writing and word processing. The driving question was that of how long the practice of having adults write or type children's dictated sentences should be continued before the children were encouraged to attempt to write on their own. In her first year of work with word processing and the new writing curriculum, Bev used dicatation to introduce her children to the concept of writing as "talk written down." She abandoned the practice early in the year when many of her children became bored with watching words appear on the computer screen and some children were able to encode some of their own words in print. In the spring, however, she recounted an observation that led her to question this decision. One of her "best writers" requested that she sit with him at the computer and type a story he wanted to tell. His story, far more rich and complex than any he had been able to write for himself, caused her to reconsider.

Perhaps we've given up dictation too soon. . . . Maybe we should be doing it with one child at a time rather than as a full group . . . as was done in the beginning of the year.

In the following year, individual children dictated sentences and stories to Bev, the researcher, and parent volunteers throughout much of the school year. As the children became more proficient in recognizing and recording letters and letter sounds and in using the computer, the practice of dictation gave way slowly and almost imperceptibly to shared writing and finally writing in which the child was the writer and the adult was a coach. As in Barbara's classroom, the evolution of coached writing represented a shift not only in the learning activities made available to children but also in the social relationships between children and adults that surrounded learning to write.

As seen in the dates on which the recurrences of Bev's questions were recorded, her attention to the role of dictation in learning to write and the possible effects of word processing on learning to print with pencils and paper was neither continuous nor singular. Other demands on her time and attention periodically drew her away from her deliberations. As a result of the ongoingness of teaching and the multiple demands it places on a teacher's time and attention, Bev's progress, like that of her colleagues, was not continuous.

Curriculum Work: Episodic vs. Continuous

The teachers' progress through their curriculum work was not steady, but discontinuous and variable, or episodic. It proceeded rapidly at times, at other times haltingly, and sometimes not at all. The teachers addressed issues related to word processing as they arose in their teaching, then set them aside when other issues became more pressing. There were periods of intense activity and thought about particular issues, then pauses of either relative satisfaction or the distraction of more pressing issues. Periods of satisfaction were rare; the ever-changing needs and strengths of the teachers' children and their own growing understanding and skill required continuous examination and revision. More often, progress was halted or slowed when the teachers' attention was diverted.

Some diversions came in the form of the day-to-day demands of maintaining ongoing classroom routines. Yearly cycles of events also diverted their time, energy, and attention. Holidays, standardized testing, and preparation for parent-teacher conferences routinely turned teachers' attention away from their work with word processing. They were further diverted by the continuous cycles of mandated curriculum change at the school-district level.

In the kindergarten, for example, where the mandated, standardized curriculum continued to become more academic, multiple diversions of energy and attention were evident. In the first two months of school, Bev's time and energy were directed toward initiating her children into the rigorous routines of an academic kindergarten that resembled, in many respects, a traditional first grade. Her time and attention were also dominated by the extensive individual evaluation of her children's skills at the beginning of the school year and again before spring parent-teacher conferences. Understandably, little progress in curriculum making and critique was made during these times. Methods of word-processing instruction and the content of that instruction, continued unchanged and unquestioned during these times.

Progress in curriculum development varied across school years as well. Margaret's first year of work with word processing, for example, was marked by significant growth in not only her pedagogical knowledge of how to teach word processing to second-grade children, but also how word processing uncovered children's previously masked abilities to edit their writing. Both the surface features and the deep structure of her teaching, in the form of assumptions about second graders as writers, were significantly altered. In the second year, however, she felt that her progress with word processing was impeded by a particularly difficult class and by the introduction of the new reading series. Given the demands placed on her time in and out of class she reported that, had that been her first year of work with word processing rather than her second, she would probably not have attempted to use word processing at all.

Margaret's second year of work with word processing coincided with Debby's first year. For Debby, it was a time of few distractions. She perceived the conditions to be right for rapid progress. First, she enjoyed the benefit of having many children in her class who had been introduced to word processing by Margaret in the previous year. Furthermore, now that she was beginning her second full year of teaching the third-grade curriculum, she felt that she had "energy" that she needed to "focus" on a task like altering her curriculum. She looked forward to the challenge of enhancing her writing curriculum and exploring word processing. The previous year, by her own report, was one of "weaving her way" through the third-grade curriculum for the first time. She had rejected the idea of introducing the children to the computer because she feared becoming "bogged down" by the additional demands it would place on her. But in the following year, she felt that she was able to begin her work with word processing with relatively few distractions and competing demands, and her work proceeded rapidly.

Implicit in all of the descriptions of the teachers' work in Part III is the influence of the surrounding contexts. The rapid and then halting progress that each teacher made can only be understood when the complex, interrelated, and sometimes conflicting contexts are taken into account.

CURRICULUM PROCESSES AND PROGRESS IN CONTEXT

The teachers' recursive and episodic processes of questioning, observing, and altering the goals, content, materials, and methods of their curricula were inextricably embedded in the histories and ideologies surrounding their work. The questions the teachers posed about curriculum, the observations they made, and the subsequent alterations they made to curricula, as well as the course and pacing of the progress of their work, must be understood within these contexts.

Ongoing policies and practices in the contexts surrounding the teachers' curriculum work defined the starting points of their work, marked the boundaries within which they could exercise their agency, and determined the time, energy, and attention they could devote to their word-processing curricula at a given point in time. Chapter 6 established the importance of the teachers' ongoing curriculum practices as foundations for the word-processing curriculum they would create. School-district curriculum policies that prescribed or failed to prescribe standardized content and practice established the boundaries of the teachers' curriculum discretion. Additionally, the multiple and often conflicting contexts surrounding the teachers' classroom curriculum work limited or made available the energy and sustained attention that the teachers required to conduct their curriculum work.

The ideologies underlying the policies and practices shaped and assigned value to the teachers' work. The teachers' values, beliefs, and goals determined what goals to strive for, and, consequently, where to focus their observations and questions. Barbara's personal, professional beliefs, values, and goals led her to pay particular attention to the potential effects of word processing on her children's self-concepts. The value Debby placed on children teaching children, that Bev placed on children learning to love coming to school, and that Margaret placed on children enjoying writing stimulated their questions, directed their observations, and influenced the alterations they made in their curricula.

Furthermore, the ideologies underlying the policies and practices in the surrounding contexts ascribed value to their work. For example, in the school, curriculum innovation was highly regarded and the teachers' work received support and respect. In the school district, the teachers' day-to-day curriculum making went unrecognized, diminishing its value in the teachers' eyes yet permitting them to proceed with their work without school-district regulation.

Teachers' individual histories of experience with curriculum work and institutional histories of policy and practice were sources of the considerable expertise the teachers brought to their work of creating word-processing curricula. The long period of laissez faire curriculum policy that preceded that of prescription and standardization provided the opportunity for the veteran teachers to hone their skills of curriculum making and critique and firmly establish active and empowered relationships with curriculum. So robust was this relationship, and so enduring were the skills, that when curriculum standardization replaced laissez faire curriculum policy, and Debby joined the faculty, that empowered relationship to curriculum still thrived in the school culture and Debby was socialized into its roles and helped to acquire the necessary skills.

SUMMARY

Embedding the processes of the teachers' work with word processing and writing curricula in their complex, evolving, and often conflicting contexts provides a frame for understanding those processes. Without an understanding of the histories and ideologies of the individuals, the institutions in which they are participants, and the dynamic interaction among them, the teachers' agency in curriculum work could be misinterpreted, or, just as serious, rendered invisible.

When seen through the eyes of the teachers themselves, and interpreted in the light of ideological and historical contexts, the processes by which the teachers created and critiqued curriculum in their own classrooms gain in stature. "Just experimenting" is understood and legitimated as focused and deliberative activity in which curriculum knowledge is created, revised, increased, and elaborated on. Halting progress is understood as a response to the multiple demands placed on teachers as they engage in curriculum making. Repeated returns to questions or issues are seen as reconsiderations in altered conditions, as well as "picking up where one left off" when attention was diverted. Finally, the teachers' inquiry is recognized as a means to and an expression of teachers' agency in relation to curriculum.

CONCLUSION

The teachers' work reported here suggests that the definition of agency proposed in Chapter 1 requires elaboration and refinement. The agency exercised by the teachers in their curriculum work varied in both organizational legitimacy and orientation. Further, the forms of agency the teachers demonstrated—and did not demonstrate—in this particular setting and at this particular time in their personal histories, and the history of the school and school district, did not represent the full range of agency that might exist. Rather, it reflected and was to some extent constrained by the complex and often conflicting contexts in which they conducted their work.

The teachers engaged in curriculum agency that was recognized and legitimized by the school district as well as agency that was conducted without its overt recognition and approval. Officially sanctioned agency, seen in the form of teacher representation on district-wide curriculum committees, was so limited in its scope that it was best characterized as false agency. Although intended to invite teachers into more professional and empowered roles in relation to curriculum, teacher representation on curriculum committees that selected or created curriculum mandated for use throughout the school district did not significantly alter teachers' curriculum work. Teacher representatives did not participate in debating or making fundamental decisions about the goals, content, or methods of the curriculum, and the majority of teachers not serving on a particular committee merely continued to receive curriculum created or selected and mandated by others.

For the most part, the teachers engaged in curriculum agency that was not officially sanctioned but was the unintended outcome of both the absence of curriculum policy and the hierarchical distance from which standardized curricula were mandated—in effect, a de facto agency. In these cases, agency was not explicitly discouraged by school district policies or practices, nor did it receive official recognition, but it was exercised in the absence of curriculum mandates and in the discretionary spaces present in the loosely coupled school system. In the period of laissez-faire curriculum policy, for example, the teachers made significant decisions about the goals, content, and materials of the curriculum in their own classrooms. In addition, individual teachers openly explored whole language instruction, process approaches to teaching writing, and computer applications. Similarly, during their participation in the research project the teachers created and critiqued word-processing curricula in the absence of a prescribed computer curriculum. Further, the teachers exercised de facto agency in the face of a district-wide standardized curriculum. Because the greatest part of the teachers' curriculum work was removed in physical and hierarchical space from those who mandated it, the teachers exercised considerable (albeit, de facto) agency as they created, altered, and critiqued curricula in their own classrooms.

The agency the teachers demonstrated can be characterized in terms of its orientation as well as its organizational legitimacy. For the most part the teachers' agency was oriented toward practical interest. As Grundy (1987) has argued, practical interest, as opposed to technical interest, is characterized by attention to making "good" curriculum decisions that value nurturing individual growth toward understanding, rather than "correct" ones that value faithful curriculum implementation. Careful deliberation and thorough understanding of the particular setting and particular learners are cornerstones of curriculum work guided by practical interest. For the teachers in this study, questions of developmental and contextual appropriateness were of central concern. Content, methods, and materials were routinely added to or rejected from curricula on the basis of their contribution to children's academic or personal growth.

The agency the teachers demonstrated did not reflect, although it did not preclude, an overtly political or critical orientation guided by emancipatory interest. Drawing again on Grundy (1987), curriculum agency grounded in emancipatory interest would base curriculum deliberation and action not only on measures of developmental and contextual appropriateness, but also on measures of social justice and equality. Grounded in the assumption that curricula are socially constructed, curriculum agency guided by emancipatory interest would question what appears to be natural or inevitable in a curriculum. It would seek out the assumptions about children, teaching, learning, schools, and society on which curricula are based, and raise questions of who benefits and who loses as a result of particular curriculum decisions.

The forms and processes of teacher agency in curriculum matters documented and analyzed here suggest directions and cautions for teachers, teacher educators, and school reformers who seek to nurture agency rather than merely expound the rhetoric of teacher empowerment. In order to nurture overt legitimized, agency that engages all teachers in questions of the values, goals, materials, and methods of curriculum, attention must be paid to the fit between the ideology of agency and the dominant ideology of the institutions in which it is to be fostered. The historical and personal contexts in which agency is to be nurtured, and the nature of the perceptions and skills each teacher brought to her agency in curriculum work must also be considered.

First, agency, as it has been defined and instantiated here, assumes particular conceptions of both curriculum and the teacher. It assumes that curriculum is mutually constructed by teachers and students through their ongoing engagement with content in a particular context, and that the teacher is a creator and critic of valid curriculum knowledge. Schools, as they are currently structured, base their curriculum policies and procedures on a strikingly different ideological base: Curriculum is assumed to be a rationalized product created by experts and generalizable across contexts. Teachers are, therefore, assumed to be consumers of curriculum knowledge but are not assumed to have requisite skills to create or critique that knowledge.

The poor fit between the assumptions underlying agency and the assumptions underlying the curriculum policies and practices of most schools has yielded such anomalies as voiceless teachers "participating" in curriculum decisions and the "empowerment" of some teachers to select or create curricula that systematically disempower their colleagues. It has also allowed teachers' active engagement with fundamental curriculum questions such as the validity of curriculum goals, the appropriateness and effectiveness of content, materials, and methods to be misperceived as recalcitrance or conservatism. The ideological walls that block true agency are those that define curriculum knowledge as a rationally created and sanctioned commodity, controlled and enforced by experts who deliver it to the masses of teachers who are assumed to be incapable or unwilling to engage in such work. In these cases, "empowering" teachers is equated with inviting selected teachers into existing hierarchical power relationships based on the creation, control, and delivery of curriculum knowledge to the many by the few.

Offering teachers a voice by merely extending their role to include "the selection of textbooks and standardized tests," as Anrig argues in his call for "teacher empowerment" (in Maeroff, 1988, p. 52), is analogous to inviting prisoners to select their own chains. Limiting teachers' participation in curriculum work to selecting packaged curricula and standardized tests, which exert technical control over their work and deskill them by separating the tasks of curricular conception and execution (Apple, 1982), is neither empowering nor educative. It contributes nothing to the introduction of teachers' voices in curriculum deliberations and nothing to the individual teacher's growth in the knowledge, skills, and attitudes required for active and effective engagement in curriculum work.

Second, teacher agency and the relationship between curriculum and teachers that it assumes cannot be viewed as ahistorical, impersonal, or decontextualized. Teachers' exercise of agency is inextricably embedded in the histories and present realities of the individual teachers and the institutions they inhabit. Therefore, it is necessary to look past surface demonstrations of compliance or resistance and to focus instead on organizational realities surrounding that behavior and teachers' perceptions of those realities. It was clear, in this study, that the teachers' perceptions of the value and limits of their own agency and the legitimacy of their own curriculum knowledge and skills were exceedingly sensitive to the influences of the overlapping and conflicting contexts in which they worked. Whether their perceptions matched those of their colleagues or of outside observers was less significant than the fact that these perceptions formed the foundations of their active and critical engagement with curriculum. It is imperative, therefore, that efforts to build upon or nurture teacher agency in curriculum matters recognize the meanings teachers ascribe to their ongoing curriculum work and to current and proposed curriculum policies. For in-service teachers, this means taking into account individual teacher's assumptions about curriculum and teachers' role as well as their professional experiences in both past and present school contexts. For preservice teachers, it means understanding their conceptions of teachers' role in curriculum as the product of years of observation and participation with teachers in their own schooling. For both in-service and preservice teachers, it means honoring these meanings and assumptions as the foundations on which to base growth toward greater agency.

Finally, each teacher in this study brought a repertoire of skills to the tasks of creating and critiquing curriculum—posing questions about the appropriateness of particular content, critiquing materials and methods to determine their potential to support goals deemed important, altering them in response to their critiques, and observing and assessing their effect with their children. It is significant that these skills were acquired in the exercise of agency in day-to-day curriculm work even in limited or nascent forms. In response to assertions that "teachers are not prepared to assume the responsibility of participation" in curriculum work and that "natural selection has operated to put those best prepared to carry the load in the positions of authority," Dewey (1937/1981) argued that teachers' "incapacity to assume the responsibilities involved in having a voice in shaping policies is bred and increased by conditions in which responsibility is denied" (p. 223). It is necessary, therefore, to identify and legitimate even the most rudimentary curriculum making or critique as holding seeds that, if nurtured, may grow into agency.

If the skills of agency are acquired through active engagement with curriculum, teacher agency must be viewed as both a means toward as well as a goal of professional development. It follows that no teacher should be prevented or discouraged from active engagement in curriculum work nor should she be left to engage in such work surreptitiously and without collegial support. Current plans to institute career ladders and professional growth paths that delay and limit teachers' engagement in curriculum work must be reconsidered and attention directed toward finding ways to support all teachers in their curriculum work throughout their careers. Rather than precluding beginning teachers' participation in curriculum deliberations and overlooking the extensive amount of creation and critique of curriculum that takes place daily in their classrooms, their most tentative or naive curriculum making or critique should be recognized as the foundation of growth toward agency. Rather than limiting the participation of more experienced teachers in sanctioned curriculum work to a select few and restricting their work to the selection of packaged curricula, consideration of the most fundamental curriculum questions of epistomology and value needs to be opened to as many teachers as possible. It should be conducted in ways that seek and honor their personal, practical, and situated knowledge accumulated and carefully honed over years. For preservice teachers, this work suggests that acquiring agency in the context of active examination, creation, and critique of curriculum means that their role in relation to curriculum must be altered—in both formal coursework and field placements—from that of passive functionary whose job it is to absorb professional knowledge and master professional skills to that of creator and critic of professional knowledge in collaboration with experienced campus-based and school-based educators.

In summary, recognition and encouragement of teacher agency in curriculum making and critique requires a major ideological shift and recognition of the significance of the personal and historical contexts of teachers' curriculum work. Nurturing teacher agency requires alignment of assumptions underlying agency and the dominant ideologies in schools, or, at the very least, recognition of the ideological distance that currently exists between the two. This is a necessary first step toward the recognition and nurturance of teacher agency. Nurturing teacher agency requires as well that teachers' curriculum work be understood in terms of its present and historical contexts and that it be interpreted through the eyes of the teachers who live it. To do so permits teachers, teacher educators, and others who would support teacher agency in curriculum matters to recognize the personal, practical, and contextualized curriculum knowledge teachers already possess, to value the processes by which they create and critique it, and be sensitive to and build upon that knowledge and those processes that may already exist within teachers' repertoires. Failure to do so may limit the achievements of reform to mere reproduction of teachers' existing relationships to curriculum.

Appendix: Methodology

This study, conducted in conjunction with the Microcomputers and Writing Development Project, was undertaken from constructivist and interpretive perspectives that assume teachers' curriculum knowledge and practice is situated, personal, and practical and is generated in the ongoing process of teaching (Connelly & Clandinin, 1985, 1988; Elbaz, 1983; Schwab, 1969; Zumwalt, 1988). Furthermore, the study was based on assumptions that teachers' curriculum knowledge and curriculum work is both shaped and given meaning by their personal images (Clandindin, 1986), personal constructs (Olson, 1980), or curriculum construct systems (Bussis, Chittenden, & Amarel, 1976), and that these personal meanings are negotiated in local contexts over time (Erickson, 1986). From this assumption of the subjectivity of experience, it follows that the meanings the teacher constructs around his or her situation may or may not match another's equally subjective view of the teacher's reality. Geertz (1973) identifies these subjective interpretations as "webs of significance" that individuals create around their experiences, and it is his interpretive approach to research that is adopted here to seek out the categories and meanings that the teachers constructed to make sense of their work with curriculum.

This study then, is an interpretation of others' realities. One cannot presume to see as another sees, but only to bring one's own experiences and understanding to, and record, what is seen. The resulting record and interpretation will only be one way of ordering and making sense of the events observed. It is constructed by the observer, a "fiction" that is, according to Geertz (1973), appropriate only if one seeks not to "capture" events but to "clarify what goes on . . . to reduce puzzlement." I do not presume to reproduce the teachers' experiences, only to shed light on them.

In keeping with this goal, and theoretical perspective, methods of data collection and analysis were grounded in ethnographic assumptions and procedures that attended to teachers' perceptions as well as practices (Erickson 1986) in multi-leveled contexts (Ogbu, 1981) that reached back into personal and institutional histories and ideologies. Long-term participant observation in the research setting and ethnographic interviewing (Mishler, 1986) yielded interpretations of the teachers' curriculum work in its complex contexts from the meaning perspectives of the participants.

153

PARTICIPANTS

Invitations to participate in the research were offered by the principal to teachers—one from each grade level from kindergarten to fourth grade—whom she perceived to be interested in participating in research on children's writing development and teachers' curriculum work. All but one of the teachers invited agreed to participate; the one who declined did so because she was unable to attend the summer workshop. The principal extended an invitation to another teacher at that grade level who subsequently agreed to participate.

One of the five participating teachers requested that her work not be included in the report of this research. The data on her work, however, remained in the data base and were included in the process of analysis (see Data Analysis below). Although her work is not represented in the classroom portraits, direct quotes, or vignettes, the impact of her computer expertise and knowledge of curriculum development, which she shared freely with her colleagues in the research project, is reflected in their work.

DATA COLLECTION

Long-term participant observation and ethnographic interviewing yielded data that documented the teachers' curriculum work from their own perspectives and set their work within its complex ideological and historical contexts. (Although national attention to the issues of accountability and school reform is an important context, systematic data collection for this study extended no further than the school district, and this analysis is therefore limited to contexts within the school district only.) Data were collected over a two-year period beginning with the teachers' first experiences with the word processors in the summer workshops, which were held the month before the beginning of each school year, and continuing through the first two years of work for three of the teachers and the first year of work for the two remaining teachers. The primary data base included field notes of classroom observations (138 entries), informal discussions with teachers (103 recorded), transcriptions of audiotaped formal interviews with individual teachers (19) and of audiotaped meetings of teachers and reseachers (10), and copies of journals kept by two of the teachers.

Classroom observations of children and teachers working with word processing took place weekly as school and university calendars permitted. Observations were scheduled during the language arts and free choice periods of the class day and lasted from 1 to 3½ hours, with most observations lasting 1 to 2 hours. I made 92 observations; 42 additional observations were recorded by my colleagues in the larger project who were assigned to the other three classrooms, and these observations were included in the data base as well.

I documented 89 informal discussions with the teachers in my field notes and reflections, and supplemented this collection with 14 additional discussions recorded in the field notes of my colleagues. Informal interviews were initiated by either the teacher or the researcher before or after a weekly observation, in weekly visits to collect journals, or when meeting by chance in hallways. These informal interviews often yielded important information about the teachers' immediate concerns.

Interviews were conducted by appointment with individual teachers at approximately the midpoint and at the end of each school year. In addition, two interviews were also conducted with the principal to supplement the informal discussions I had had with her in hallways and classrooms. Each interview lasted from ½ to 1½ hours and was audiotaped and transcribed. Although for each interview specific questions were prepared to explore more deeply the themes and issues that had been raised in group meetings or suggested in teachers' journals, informal discussions, or classroom observations, the teachers used the interviews as opportunities to share their reactions to immediate situations and relate those experiences to other experiences and, in effect, to "tell their stories" (Erickson, 1986; Mishler, 1986). Formal interview questions were most often attended to briefly; the greatest part of each interview was devoted to the effort of the teacher and the researcher to negotiate their individual understandings of the teacher's experience of immediate classroom situations.

Proceedings of 10 group meetings were audiotaped and transcribed. These meetings, held five times each school year, lasted from 1 hour to 1½ hours. The meetings were devoted to each teacher's descriptions of her progress with the curriculum and her children's progress since the previous meeting, to the teachers' responses to questions posed by the researchers, and to discussions of hardware, software, record keeping, scheduling, or funding concerns initiated by the teachers or the researchers.

The teachers were asked to keep journals to which I would respond. They were asked to write daily entries during a summer workshop and weekly entries through the school year. Although all of the teachers wrote during the summer workshop week, keeping a weekly journal through the school year proved to be excessively time-consuming, and in the end only two teachers wrote with regularity for some or most of their first year.

DATA ANALYSIS

The qualitative methods used to analyze the corpus of data included content analysis and the identification of typical and discrepant cases using the methods of analytic induction and triangulation. Field notes, teachers' journals, and transcriptions of audiotaped meetings and interviews from work with all five of the teachers were compiled chronologically, yielding a "contour" or shape of the teachers' curriculum work and making it possible to track individual teachers' practices and concerns over time. Analysis began with the first meeting with the teachers and continued throughout the two years of data collection.

Several tools served as "conceptual levers" (Schatzman & Strauss, 1973) throughout the analysis. First, socially constructed definitions used by administrators and teachers to describe critical concepts such as "good teacher" or "colleague" provided one view of the meanings attached to events and behaviors in the process of curriculum change. Grace (1978) argues that a school's ethos or dominant assumptions are revealed by such definitions. These shared definitions, remarkably consistent within groups, showed how participants understood their roles in curriculum work. Second, metaphors were used, as Lakoff and Johnson (1980) suggest, as "important tools for trying to comprehend partially what cannot be comprehended totally" (p. 193). The metaphors teachers and adminstrators used to describe their experiences shed light on how they understood those experiences. Third, "theories-in-use" (Argyris & Schon, 1974) or beliefs, values, and assumptions inferred from patterns of behavior were sought in the policies and practices of administrators, teachers, and researchers. Finally, the expectations that the teachers held about how curriculum work should proceed provided another window on the beliefs that undergirded their experiences. According to Rokeach (1968), "beliefs are inferences made by observers about the underlying state of expectancy" (p. 2). Expectations were reflected in the teachers' behavior in their first encounters with the researchers, in much the same way that Berreman (1962) found that "initial responses to an ethnographer by his subjects is probably always an attempt to identify him in familiar roles" (p. 13).

Inferences and interpretations that were products of the use of these "conceptual levers" guided each subsequent consideration of the full data base, which included the work of the fifth teacher. In order to prevent each return to the data from becoming an exercise in post hoc substantiation of foregone conclusions, each return to the data was used to search for contradictions that would lead to modification or rejection of an inference, pattern, or theme as well as to search for data to support or extend it. Rereadings of the data continued, as robust inferences were strengthened and weak inferences were altered or eliminated, until subsequent readings of the data yielded no further substantiation or contradiction.

References

Amarel, M. (1983). Classrooms and computers as instructional settings. *Theory into Practice, 22,* 260–266.

Apple, M. W. (1979). *Ideology and the curriculum.* London: Routledge & Kegan Paul.

Apple, M. W. (1982). *Education and power.* London: Routledge & Kegan Paul.

Apple, M. W. (1983). Curricular form and the logic of technical control. In M. W. Apple & L. Weiss (Eds.), *Ideology and practice in schooling* (pp. 143–165). Philadelphia: Temple University Press.

Apple, M. W. (1986). *Teachers and texts.* London: Routledge & Kegan Paul.

Apple, M. W., & Jungck, S. (1990). "You don't have to be a teacher to teach this unit": Teaching, technology and gender in the classroom. *American Educational Research Journal, 27*(2), 227–251.

Apple, M. W., & Teitelbaum, K. (1986). "Are teachers losing control of their skills and curriculum?" *Journal of Curriculum and Supervision, 18*(2), 177–184.

Arendt, H. (1958). *The human condition.* Chicago: University of Chicago Press.

Argyris, C., & Schön, D. (1974). *Theory in practice.* San Francisco: Jossey–Bass.

Bastian, A., Fruchter, N., Gittel, M., Greer, C., & Haskins, K. (1986). *Choosing equality: The case for democratic schooling.* Philadelphia: Temple University Press.

Bateson, M. C. (1990). *Composing a life.* New York: Penguin.

Ben-Peretz, M. (1990). *The teacher–curriculum encounter: Freeing teachers from the tyranny of texts.* Albany: State University of New York Press.

Berman, P., & McLaughlin, M. W. (1978). *Federal programs supporting educational change: Vol. 8. Implementing and sustaining innovations.* Santa Monica, CA: Rand Corporation.

Berreman, G. (1962). *Behind many masks* (Monograph No. 4). Ithaca, NY: Society for Applied Anthropology.

Bissex, G. L., & Bullock, R. H. (1987). *Seeing for ourselves: Case-study research by teachers of writing.* Portsmouth, NH: Heinemann Educational Books.

Bobbitt, F. (1926). The orientation of the curriculum maker. In G. Whipple (Ed.), *The foundations and technique of curriculum construction, Part II. Twenty-sixth yearbook of the National Society for the Study of Education* (pp. 41–55). Bloomington, IL: Public School Publishing.

Britton, J. (1987). A quiet form of research. In D. Goswami & P. Stillman (Eds.), *Reclaiming the classroom* (pp. 13–19). Upper Montclair, NJ: Boynton/Cook.

Brown, J., Collins, A., & Duguid, P. (1989). Situated cognition and the culture of learning. *Educational Researcher, 18*(1), 34–41.

Bruce, B., Michaels, S., & Watson-Gegeo, K. (1985). How computers can change the writing process. *Language Arts, 62,* 143–149.

Bureau of the Census. (1987). *Statistical abstract of the United States* (107th ed.). Washington, DC: U.S. Department of Commerce.

Bussis, A., Chittenden, E., & Amarel, M. (1976). *Beyond surface curriculum.* Boulder, CO: Westview Press.

Calkins, L. (1983). *Lessons from a child.* Portsmouth, NH: Heinemann Educational Books.

Calkins, L. (1986). *The art of teaching writing.* Portsmouth, NH: Heinemann Educational Books.

Carnegie Forum on Education and the Economy. (1986). *A nation prepared.* New York: Carnegie Corporation.

Clandinin, J. (1986). *Classroom practice.* Philadelphia: Falmer Press.

Cochran-Smith, M. (1984). *The making of a reader.* Norwood, NJ: Ablex Publishing.

Cochran-Smith, M. (1991). Word processing and writing. *Review of Educational Research, 61*(1), 107–155.

Cochran-Smith, M., Kahn, J. K., & Paris, C. L. (1990). When microcomputers come into the classroom. In S. Silvern & J. Hoot (Eds.), *Word processing in the elementary school* (pp. 43–74). New York: Teachers College Press.

Cochran-Smith, M., & Lytle, S. L. (1988). Research on teaching and teacher research: The issues that divide. *Educational Researcher, 19,* 2–11.

Cochran-Smith, M., & Lytle, S. L. (1993). *Inside/outside: Teacher research and knowledge.* New York: Teachers College Press.

Cochran–Smith, M., Paris, C. L., & Kahn, J. K. (1991). *Learning to write differently: Beginning writers and word processing.* Norwood, NJ: Ablex Publishing.

Colletti, J. (1987). *Professional development: A dialectic process of thought and action.* Unpublished manuscript.

Committee on Curriculum-Making. (1926). A composite statement by the members of the society's committee on curriculum-making. In G. Whipple (Ed.), *The foundations and technique of curriculum construction, Part II. Twenty–sixth yearbook of the National Society for the Study of Education* (pp. 11–28). Bloomington, IL: Public School Publishing.

Connell, R. W. (1985). *Teachers' work.* N. Sydney, Australia: George Allen & Unwin.

Connelly, E. M., & Clandinin, D. J. (1985). Personal practical knowledge and the modes of knowing: Relevance for teaching and learning. In E. Eisner (Ed.), *Learning and teaching the ways of knowing* (pp. 174–198). Chicago: University of Chicago Press.

Connelly, E. M., & Clandinin, D. J. (1988). *Teachers as curriculum planners: Narratives of experience.* New York: Teachers College Press.

Cuban, L. (1984). *How teachers taught: Constancy and change in American classrooms 1890–1980.* New York: Longman.

Cuban, L. (1986). *Teachers and machines: The classroom use of technology since 1920.* New York: Teachers College Press.

Dewey, J. (1916). *Democracy and education.* New York: Free Press.

Dewey, J. (1981). Democracy and educational administration. In *Later works* (Vol. 11, pp. 217–225). Carbondale: Southern Illinois University Press. (Original work published 1937)

Dickinson, D. (1986). Integrating computers into a first and second grade writing program. *Research in the Teaching of English, 20,* 357–378.

Doyle, W. (1979). Making managerial decisions in classrooms. In D. L. Duke (Ed.), *Seventy-eighth annual yearbook of the National Society for the Study of Education* (pp. 42–74). Chicago: University of Chicago Press.

Doyle, W. (1983). Academic work. *Review of Research in Education, 53*(2),159–199.

Doyle, W., & Ponder, G. A. (1977). The practicality ethic in teacher decision–making. *Interchange, 8*(3), 1–12.

Duckworth, E. (1986). Teaching as research. *Harvard Educational Review, 56*(4), 481–495.

Eisner, E. (1981). On the differences between scientific and aesthetic approaches to qualitative research. *Educational Researcher, 10,* 5–9.

Elbaz, F. (1983). *Teacher thinking: A study of practical knowledge.* New York: Nichols Publishing.

Erickson, F. (1986). Qualitative methods in research on teaching. In M. Wittrock (Ed.), *Handbook of research on teaching* (3rd ed., pp. 109–161). New York: Macmillan.

Feiman-Nemser, S., & Floden, R. E. (1986). The cultures of teaching. In M. Wittrock (Ed.), *Handbook of research on teaching* (3rd ed., pp. 505–526). New York: Macmillan.

Freedman, S. E. (1988). Teaching, gender, and curriculum. In L. Beyer & M. Apple (Eds.), *The curriculum: Problems, politics, possibilities* (pp. 204–218). Albany: State University of New York Press.

Fullan, M. (1982). *The meaning of educational change.* New York: Teachers College Press.

Futrell, M. H. (1986). Restructuring teaching: A call for research. *Educational Researcher, 15*(9), 5–8.

Geertz, C. (1973). *The interpretation of cultures.* New York: Basic Books.

Gianquinta, J. B. (1973). The process of organizational change in schools. In F. N. Kerlinger (Ed.), *Review of research in education* (Vol. 1, pp. 178–208). Itasca, IL: F. E. Peacock.

Ginsburg, M. (1988). *Contradictions in teacher education and society: A critical analysis.* Philadelphia: Falmer Press.

Gitlin, A. (1983). School structure and teacher's work. In M. Apple & L. Weiss (Eds.), *Ideology and practice in schooling* (pp. 193–212). Philadelphia: Temple University Press.

Glatthorn, A. (1987). *Curriculum leadership.* Glenview, IL: Scott, Foresman.

Goodlad, J. I., Klein, M. F., & Tye, K. A. (1979). The domains of curriculum and their study. In J. Goodlad (Ed.), *Curriculum inquiry* (pp. 43–76). New York: McGraw-Hill.

Goswami, D., & Stillman, P. R. (1987). *Reclaiming the classroom: Teacher research as an agency for change.* Upper Montclair, NJ: Boyton Cook.

Grace, G. (1978). *Teachers, ideology and control: A study in urban education.* Boston: Routledge & Kegan Paul.

Graves, D. (1983). *Writing: Teachers and children at work.* Portsmouth, NH: Heinemann Educational Books.

Green, J. (1983). Research on teaching as a linguistic process: A state of the art. In E. W. Gordon (Ed.), *Review of research in education* (Vol. 10, pp. 151–252). Washington, DC: American Educational Research Association.

Greene, M. (1978a). *Landscapes of learning*. New York: Teachers College Press.

Greene, M. (1978b). Teaching and the question of personal reality. *Teachers College Record, 80*, 23–35.

Gross, N., Gianquinta, J. B., & Bernstein, M. (1971). *Implementing organizational innovations*. New York: Basic Books.

Grundy, S. (1987). *Curriculum: Product or praxis*. Philadelphia: Falmer Press.

Hawkins, J., & Sheingold, K. (1986). The beginning of a story: Computers and the organization of learning in classrooms. In J. Albertson & L. Cunningham (Eds.), *Microcomputers and education. Eighty-fifth yearbook of the National Society for the Study of Education* (pp. 40–58). Chicago: University of Chicago Press.

Heath, S. B. (1982). *Ways with words*. New York: Cambridge University Press.

Holmes Group. (1986). *Tomorrow's teachers*. East Lansing, MI: Author.

Huberman, M., & Miles, M. (1984). *Innovation up close*. New York: Plenum Press.

Huling-Austin, L. (1990). Teacher induction programs and internships. In R. Houston (Ed.), *Handbook of research on teacher education* (pp. 535–548). New York: Macmillan.

Judd, C. H. (1926). Supplementary statement. In G. Whipple (Ed.), *The foundations and technique of curriculum construction, Part II. Twenty-sixth yearbook of the National Society for the Study of Education* (pp. 113–117). Bloomington, IL: Public School Publishing.

Kahn, J. (1988). *Learning to write with a new tool: A study of emergent writers using word processing*. Unpublished doctoral dissertation, University of Pennsylvania, Philadelphia.

Kerr, D. (1987). Authority and responsibility in public schooling. In J. Goodlad (Ed.), *The ecology of school renewal* (pp. 20–40). Chicago: National Society for the Study of Education.

Kilpatrick, W. H. (1923). Introduction. In E. Collings, *An experiment with a project curriculum* (pp. xvii–xxvi). New York: Macmillan.

Kilpatrick, W. H. (1926). Statement of position. In G. Whipple (Ed.), *The foundations and technique of curriculum construction, Part II. Twenty-sixth yearbook of the National Society for the Study of Education* (pp. 119–146). Bloomington, IL: Public School Publishing.

Kliebard, H. (1987). *Struggle for the American curriculum 1893–1958*. Boston: Routledge & Kegan Paul.

Lakoff, G., & Johnson, M. (1980). *Metaphors we live by*. Chicago: University of Chicago Press.

Lampert, M. (1985). How do teachers manage to teach? Perspectives on problems in practice. *Harvard Educational Review, 55*, 178–194.

Leiberman, A., & Miller, L. (1984). *Teachers, their world and their work*. Alexandria, VA: Association for Supervision and Curriculum Development.

Lightfoot, S. L. (1983). *The good high school: Portraits of character and culture*. New York: Basic Books.

Little, J. W. (1982). Norms of collegiality and experimentation: Workplace conditions of school success. *American Educational Research Journal, 19*(3), 325–340.

Lortie, D. (1975). *Schoolteacher*. Chicago: University of Chicago Press.

McDonald, J. P. (1988). The emergence of the teacher's voice: Implications for the new reform. *Teachers College Record, 89*(4), 471–487.

McLaughlin, M. W. (1976). Implementation as mutual adaptation: Change in classroom organization. *Teachers College Record, 77*(3), 339–351.

Maeroff, G. (1988). *The empowerment of teachers: Overcoming the crisis of confidence.* New York: Teachers College Press.

Mayhew, K. C., & Edwards, A. C. (1936). *The Dewey School*. New York: Appleton-Century.

Michaels, S., & Bruce, B. (1989). *Classroom contexts and literacy development: How writing systems shape the teaching and learning of composition* (Tech. Rep. No. 476). Champaign, IL: University of Illinois.

Miles, M. (1964). *Innovation in education*. New York: Teachers College Press.

Mishler, E. (1986). *Research interviewing: Context and narrative*. Cambridge, MA: Harvard University Press.

Mohr, M., & MacLean, M. (1987). *Working together*. Urbana, IL: National Council of Teachers of English.

National Coalition of Advocates for Students. (1985). *Barriers to excellence: Our children at risk*. Boston: Author.

National Commission on Excellence in Education. (1983). *A nation at risk*. Cambridge, MA: USA Research.

National Governors' Association. (1986). *A time for results: The governors' 1991 report on education*. Washington, DC: Author.

Newlon, J., & Threlkeld, A. (1926). The Denver curriculum revision program. In G. Whipple (Ed.), *The foundations and technique of curriculum construction, Part I. Twenty-sixth yearbook of the National Society for the Study of Education* (pp. 229–240). Bloomington, IL: Public School Publishing.

Newman, J. (Ed.). (1990). *Finding our own way: Teachers exploring their assumptions*. Portsmouth, NH: Heinemann Educational Books.

Ogbu, J. (1981). School ethnography: A multilevel approach. *Anthropology & Education Quarterly, 12*(1), 3–29.

Olson, J. (1980). Teacher constructs and curriculum change. *Journal of Curriculum Studies, 12*(1), 1–11.

Olson, J. (1986). *Curriculum change and classroom order*. Paper presented at the annual meeting of the American Educational Research Association, San Francisco, CA.

Olson, J. (1988). *Schoolworlds, microworlds: Computers and the culture of the classroom*. Elmsford, NY: Pergamon Press.

Papert, S. (1980). *Mindstorms*. New York: Basic Books.

Polanyi, M. (1969). *Knowing and being*. London: Routledge & Kegan Paul.

Rokeach, M. (1968). *Beliefs, attitudes and values: A theory of organizational change*. San Francisco: Jossey-Bass.

Romberg, T. A. (1988). Can teachers be professionals? In D. A. Grouws & T. J. Cooney (Eds.), *Perspectives on research on effective mathematics teaching* (Vol. 1, pp. 224–244). Reston, VA: National Council of Teachers of Mathematics.

Rosow, J. M., & Zager, R. (1989). *Allies in educational reform*. San Francisco: Jossey-Bass.

Rudduck, J., & Hopkins, D. (1985). *Research as a basis for teaching: Readings from the works of Lawrence Stenhouse*. London: Heinemann Educational Books.

Rugg, H. (1926). Curriculum-making: Points of emphasis. In G. Whipple (Ed.), *The foundations and technique of curriculum construction, Part II. Twenty-sixth yearbook of the National Society for the Study of Education* (pp. 147–162). Bloomington, IL: Public School Publishing.

Sarason, S. B. (1971). *The culture of school and the problem of change*. New York: Allyn & Bacon.

Schatzman, L., & Strauss, A. (1973). *Field research: Strategies for a natural sociology*. Englewood Cliffs, NJ: Prentice Hall.

Schön, D. A. (1983). *The reflective practitioner*. New York: Basic Books.

Schwab, J. J. (1969). The practical: A language for curriculum. *School Review, 78*, 1–23.

Scribner, S. (1984). Studying working intelligence. In B. Rogoff & B. J. Lave (Eds.), *Everyday cognition: Its development in social context* (pp. 9–40). Cambridge, MA: Harvard University Press.

Shanker, A. (1986). Teachers must take charge. *Educational Leadership, 44*(1), 12–13.

Sheingold, K., Hawkins, J., & Char, C. (1984). *I'm the thinkist you're the typist: The interaction of technology and the social life of classrooms* (Tech. Rep. No. 27). New York: Bank Street College of Education.

Shulman, L. S. (1987). Knowledge and teaching: Foundations of the new reform. *Harvard Educational Review, 57*(1), 1–22.

Silberman, C. (1970). *Crisis in the classroom: The remaking of American education*. New York: Random House.

Sizer, T. (1984). *Horace's compromise*. Boston: Houghton Mifflin.

Smith, F. (1986). *Insult to intelligence: The bureaucratic invasion of our classrooms*. New York: Arbor House.

Smith, L., & Geoffrey, W. (1968). *The complexities of the urban classroom*. New York: Holt, Rinehart & Winston.

Snyder, J., Bolin, F., & Zumwalt, K. (1992). Curriculum implementation. In P. Jackson (Ed.). *Handbook of research on curriculum* (pp. 402–435). New York: Macmillan.

Stellar, A. (1983). Curriculum planning. In F. W. English (Ed.), *Fundamental curriculum decisions*. Alexandria, VA: Association for Supervision and Curriculum Development.

Sternberg, R. J., & Caruso, D. (1985). Practical modes of knowing. In E. Eisner (Ed.), *Learning and teaching the ways of knowing* (pp. 133–158). Chicago: University of Chicago Press.

Stodolsky, S. (1989). Is teaching really by the book? In P. Jackson & S. Haroutunian-Gordon (Eds.), *From Socrates to software: The teacher as text and the text as teacher. Eighty-ninth yearbook of the National Society for the Study of Education*. Chicago: University of Chicago Press.

Stone, L. (1988). *Resisting resistance*. Paper presented at the College and University Faculty Assembly of the National Council for the Social Studies, Orlando, FL.

Sullivan, L. (1975). Urban school decentralization and curriculum development: Views and implications. In I. Staples (Ed.), *Impact of decentralization on curriculum:*

Selected viewpoints (pp. 14–17). Washington, DC: Association for Supervision and Curriculum Development.

Taylor, R. (1980). *The computer in the school: Tutor, tool, and tutee.* New York: Teachers College Press.

Tikunoff, W. J., & Mergendoller, J. R. (1983). Inquiry as a means of professional growth: The teacher as researcher. In G. Griffin (Ed.), *Staff development: 82nd yearbook of the National Society for the Study of Education* (pp. 210–227). Chicago: University of Chicago Press.

Walker, W. (1978). Education's new movement—privatism. *Educational Leadership, 35*(6), 472.

Washburne, C. W., & Marland, S. P. (1963). *The history and significance of an educational experiment.* Englewood Cliffs, NJ: Prentice Hall.

Weick, K. (1976). Educational organizations as loosely coupled systems. *Administrative Science Quarterly, 21,* 1–14.

Weizenbaum, J. (1976). *Computer power and human reason.* San Francisco: W. H. Freeman.

Wise, A. (1979). *Legislated learning: The bureaucratization of the American classroom.* Berkeley: University of California Press.

Wise, A. (1988). The two conflicting trends in school reform: Legislated learning revisited. *Phi Delta Kappan, 69,* 328–332.

Yonemura, M., Colletti, J., & Collins, J. (1986). *One early childhood educator: Implications for the professional development of teachers.* New York: Teachers College Press.

Zumwalt, K. (1988). Are we improving or undermining teaching? In L. Tanner (Ed.), *Critical issues in curriculum* (pp. 148–174). Chicago: University of Chicago Press.

Index

About the Author

Cynthia Paris is Assistant Professor of Education at Rider College in Lawrenceville, New Jersey. She received her doctorate from the University of Pennsylvania, where she has just completed a year as Visiting Assistant Professor in the Graduate School of Education. She is co-author of *Learning to Write Differently: Beginning Writers and Word Processing* (Ablex) and is currently conducting research on teachers' growth toward agency and the role of mentoring in that growth.